THE LAST GENTLEMAN

All good wishes David Niven

THE LAST GENTLEMAN

A Tribute to

David Niven

Peter Haining

W.H. ALLEN · LONDON
A Howard & Wyndham Company

Copyright © Peter Haining 1984

Phototypeset by Avocet Ltd, Aylesbury, Bucks.
Printed and bound in Great Britain by
Anchor Brendon Ltd, Tiptree, Essex
for the Publishers W. H. Allen & Co Ltd,
44 Hill Street, London W1X 8LB

ISBN 0 491 03103 3 (W. H. Allen hardcover edition)
ISBN 0 86379 042 9 (Comet Books softcover edition)

For

RALPH FIELDS

– who first flew the balloon

&

DAVID NIVEN Jnr

– who helped bring on the horses

David Niven

Born: 1 March 1910   Died: 29 July 1983

'I see my purpose in life as making the world a happier place to be in.'

'David never claimed to be a great actor although Hollywood never stretched his acting abilities to the limit. He was a lovely man and a great prankster.'
Peter Ustinov

'Working with David Niven was the only time I ever looked forward to filming. I just couldn't wait to wake up each morning and go to work so he could make me laugh.'
Marlon Brando

'I agree with the words of John Kenneth Galbraith that David Niven was the least boring man I ever met.'
Richard Burton

'I loved David for his friendship, his relish for life, his humour and his intelligence.'
Elizabeth Taylor

'David's wonderful spirit will be missed by all who knew him. He was a great friend.'
James Stewart

'It was so much better that he should have been able to die with dignity in the place he loved than in some hospital. His passing takes something irreplaceable from all our lives.'
Roger Moore

Contents

Mr David Niven

The debonair
Niv – a caricature
by Mark Boxer.

Introduction

IT WAS THE director John Huston who remarked with the delightful dry wit for which he was famous, 'My definition of hell is listening to actors talking seriously about their work.' The one person whom he could scarcely ever have accused of such a thing was David Niven, and it is perhaps not surprising, therefore, to learn that these two men were friends for most of their lives.

But in this fact lies the curious enigma of arguably the longest film career of this century. For while other actors, many of them more talented – as David would have been the first to admit – blazed across the screen, talked and worried endlessly about their craft, and yet still fell into obscurity, he outstayed them all with hardly an anguished word spoken in fifty years. For David, his work and his life were all about having a good time. He may have had his troubles, his private griefs, but his good humour remained indomitable throughout all the years of his remarkable career.

As a man who went into the movies in the thirties when he found himself by chance in Hollywood, he seemingly broke all the rules and yet survived and prospered. He appeared in over ninety films (probably more if you count his appearances as an 'extra'), created an image that the changing times *should* have made redundant but never could, and believed quite sincerely that it was all due to a modest ability and an enormous amount of luck.

The truth is, I think, that David Niven – or Niv as he liked to be known – was actually bigger than any role he was asked to take on or any part life called upon him to play. It is not easy to define the word 'bigger', but certainly where so many actors have ultimately proved to be little people attempting to fill what may well have been impossible roles thrust upon them, David was . . . David. And that was his great strength. For while these others struggled to be someone else, David employed his debonair looks and urbane manner, his wit and charm, his apparently effortless ease with people, and his unique ability as a raconteur, as the basis on which he built both his private and public life. It was what *he* wanted. And he was never in any doubt what *that* was.

'Considering the average gifts I've been given,' he confessed in 1978 without a trace of false modesty, 'I think I've done quite well. Ninety-nine per cent of people are stuck in work they hate and I've adored every minute of my job. I've been able to work when I like at what I loved, visit lovely and exciting places, be beautifully paid for having fun. And this has spoiled me rotten.'

'Spoiled' is not, though, the adjective most people would choose to describe David Niven. And indeed when one examines the ups and downs of his career, it is not difficult to see that he had to work hard for his undoubted status in the film industry. He still insisted, however, that it was all down to good luck.

'Movie acting is rather like a children's game,' he observed just a few years back. 'The difficult thing is to have good luck, or to recognise good luck when it comes. When I was an extra in Hollywood, there were 22,000 of us looking for jobs. To claw your way out of that situation your luck had to be pretty astronomical. I *am* lucky. Movies are marvellous if you're lucky. If not, they are absolute hell. And I never went to acting school, I learned my craft actually doing the work.'

Niv believed his luck amounted to being in the right place (Hollywood) at the right time (in the thirties) and acquiring some influential friends who looked out for him (the Fairbanks, father and son, Errol Flynn and Humphrey Bogart are just four of those he persistently mentioned).

'All that good luck meant I achieved something that sounds rude but isn't – audience penetration. That means you're as well known in Japan as you are in Great Britain. But,' and he would pause and smile, 'that doesn't always mean you get a job!'

Niv was never anything other than totally objective about his acting. 'I don't call acting work,' he would say. 'Eight hours at the coalface is work. Acting is just another way of having fun. My acting talent is extremely moderate and usually called upon to produce an officer, a duke or a crook.

'At the risk of sounding bombastic, I can put it this way: scripts with a

David Niven-type often come my way. To be fair, I play them as well as anybody. It has been rather incredible that I've survived as long as I have in a rapidly declining business. You're always expecting a little man in a bowler hat to come up behind you and tap you on the shoulder and say, ''You've been found out.'' An actor always has a huge inferiority complex. With good reason. It's nine-to-one against a hit. How a beginner begins these days I don't know. You press on, you do your best. Stomach in. Chest out. Doing the best you can.'

And after any such conversation which he thought seemed getting a mite serious, he could never help adding as a kind of afterthought (though it never was), 'Actors never retire, you know – they just get fewer scripts. I'm just grateful that a certain number kept coming to me!'

It would be quite wrong, however, to think that David found acting as effortless as his manner on the screen would have the viewer believe. In a rare moment of confession he told one of his closest journalist friends, Margaret Hinxman, 'The truth is when I'm working I'm not relaxed at all. Just feel my hands: they are wet with sweat. Not only during each take but all the time. It is sheer fear. That is why I pace up and down so much before I go on the set and behave like a gibbering idiot. I get so frightened that my lips go white and I always have to have some grease in a tube to put on them when they stick to the upper gum showing all my teeth!'

Niv believed the essence of a good actor was being an extrovert. 'Unless you like to pull out your extro and vert it, you wouldn't be in the business, even if you're a villain.' Successful extrovert though he was, there were still some other people David Niven wished he had been, as he told another reporter in 1959. 'I wish,' he confessed 'with all my heart that I had been born a really flamboyant character like Humphrey Bogart or Frank Sinatra. I honestly think the rest of us, the whole damn movie business, should go down on our knees to the Garbos and the Bogarts and the Sinatras and the Wallace Beerys. Because it is their flamboyance and their glamour that have kept Hollywood going – that have kept us all going.'

There are some of Niv's friends who have suggested that behind the flamboyance there lurked a shy man. But all are agreed that he was a very perceptive person with a compulsion to entertain. 'He really did have superb perceptions about people,' one intimate told me, 'even about people he met for the first time. Women in particular loved him because he knew exactly what to say to them. And the only men who ever avoided him were those who were jealous of his *joie de vivre*. In public he was always on, always playing the jester. As soon as he met someone he was off, entertaining, making them feel better. He didn't perform to be the centre of attention, though, but to cheer people up and make them happy.'

This is an assessment I do not think Niv would have denied. Indeed, he once admitted, 'I really think the key to actors is that they want to be liked. Not only for their work, but also for themselves. I developed a built-in desire to be liked. I was always performing, in school, in the Army. It's a terrible trap really, but the instinct's too strong.'

It would be wrong to think that this instinct made him in any way shallow, for his relationships with those close to him were deeply rooted and his commitment to his family and friends as well as to his convictions were unswerving. His explanation as to why he never gave up his British citizenship despite having lived abroad for much of his life graphically underlined this.

'All the time I was in Hollywood I was under pressure to become an American citizen,' he said. 'But I never did. I stayed English. I believe it's who you are that counts, not the colour of your passport. I remember some very significant lines written by Erich Maria Remarque. One character asked another, "Do you like the Germans?" No, was the reply. "Do you like the French?" No, again. "Do you like the English?" Again the reply was no. "Then who do you like?" "I like my friends," was the answer. And that's my answer, too.'

The corner-stones of David's life were, of course, his two marriages. The first, to Primula 'Primmie' Rollo, an English aristocrat's daughter, which ended in her tragic death not long after she had joined him in Hollywood. The second, to a Swedish model, Hjordis Tersmeden, bridged the years of his rise to stardom. 'On both occasions,' he would recall, 'I met and married within ten days. There was no wavering . . . I just went straight in. And the strange thing is Hjordis and Primmie have become one person for me. They are totally different, yet . . .'

From his first marriage David had two sons, David Jnr and Jamie, while he and Hjordis adopted two daughters, Kristina and Fiona.

'I've always liked women,' he said on another occasion, 'and some have liked me. The danger of being an actor is that actresses tend to be more seductive than traffic wardens. But I've always dodged the entanglements. One wife is worth more than a hundred starlets.'

'Home' to Niv was two lovely houses in France and Switzerland between which he, Hjordis and the family divided their time when he was not working. Each catered to his two greatest pastimes: skiing and sailing. His Swiss chalet home, *Château d'Oex* at Vaud, was the base he used each winter for skiing. He belonged to what he described as the exclusive 'DNO Ski Club' (David Niven's Own). The club badge – so rumour had it – was a large ham on skis, and Niv was the club's president, secretary and only champion.

For the summer months he would move to *Lo Scoglitto* (The Little Rock), a palatial pink and white villa perched on Cap Ferrat with a breathtaking view across one of the few remaining unspoiled stretches of the Côte d'Azur.

In this retreat surrounded by cyprus trees as well as a grove of 2000-year-old olive trees, the Niven family would sunbathe, swim in their heated swimming pool, or else sail the sloop or catamaran berthed in their private harbour below.

These were the fruits of Niv's hard work — and during the later years of his life he planned his work schedule to make the very best of them, never losing sight of his intention to keep life fun. He once explained how he achieved

this. 'Whenever I am offered a part in a film,' he said, 'I ask four questions. The first is, "Where is the film going to be made?" If I like the sound of the answer, I ask, "Who is going to be in it with me?" If I like the people concerned, I go on to question number three: "When is it being shot?" That is terribly important because I don't want my work to interfere with my skiing – which rules out winter filming. And I don't much like working in the summer or spring when I can sail, which really only leaves the autumn. And

Niv the storyteller – an intimate off-set picture of David entertaining two fellow film stars, Shirley Maclaine and Tony Randall.

then there is the fourth question: "How much will I be paid?" Which is crucial because I have an expensive lifestyle to maintain. So you see my career decisions have not exactly been based on artistic integrity, which accounts for the fact that so many movies I made turned out to be crummy.'

The quality of David's films is, to be sure, uneven, and more than one critic has said that while his name may be big in film terms his actual accomplishments on the screen are somewhat smaller, considering the number of pictures he made. Yet in very few of these movies does he give a *bad* performance; while those performers around him may have varied from the indifferent to the excruciating, Niv was always professional, always watchable and always *enjoyable*.

The key to this lay, I think, in his attitude, as his friend the film actor Anthony Quayle explained recently. 'David Niven was a professional at being an amateur,' he said, 'which is a very English attitude to have. It is a big pose with us that we are really only amateurs at anything. But actually we sharpen our knives and our skates and everything else we've got and we're really as hard and competitive as anybody. But Niv covered it all up with, "My Dear Old Bean – it doesn't really *matter*." He was the first person I think I ever heard when people got uptight during the making of a film who would say, "Don't worry. It's only a film!" Of course, it *was* only a film. But underneath he took it very seriously.

'As far as his career went he didn't tackle the Himalayas, if I can put it that way. He was very content to have a lot of fun on the nursery slopes. Niv was too modest for the heights – and it was also too damn cold up there as well as there being the risk of breaking your neck! So it was the nursery slopes, thank you very much. The snow was easier to fall on and there were good pickings to be made. And he made no bones about it: he wasn't there to be a great big serious actor!'

David was, as he said, afraid that he might one day be 'found out', yet even in the unlikely event that the demand for his film services had ever ceased, the sudden and astonishing success he enjoyed in the seventies when he turned writer, added a new dimension to his life and prospects. For as he later admitted, the royalties from his books, *The Moon's a Balloon*, published in 1971, and its successor in 1975, *Bring On the Empty Horses*, 'made me more money than ten movies.'

The success of these two volumes – and the third, a novel *Go Slowly, Come Back Quickly*, published in 1981 – certainly surprised the literary world, not to mention the film business and even Niv himself. Perhaps only the millions of people who had enjoyed his films, delighted in reading the endless anecdotes with which he regaled journalists, and been spellbound by his virtuoso performances as a raconteur on television, were not surprised. *They* had waited a long time for these books – the distillation of his hilarious life – and showed it by the enormous sales which resulted.

In actual fact, David had been writing since his youth. He had contributed to school magazines, written concert sketches while in the Army, and was briefly a newspaper correspondent during his early days in Hollywood. And he had even written a comic novel, *Round the Ragged Rocks*, which was published in 1951. He also excelled as a letter writer, and many friends and admirers around the world still retain treasured correspondence from Niv, handwritten in his unmistakable style and punctuated with his delightful wit.

In 1969 I remember he bemoaned to his friend Roderick Mann that the art of letter-writing seemed to have disappeared. He told him, 'I'm a great letter-writer myself, but the only other people still at it seem to be men about to be hanged or electrocuted; one's always reading their letters reprinted in the Sunday papers.'

It is true that his early literary endeavours did not set the world on fire: his newspaper column stopped after a few weeks (mainly by his own inclination) and he was actively discouraged by some friends from publishing *Round the Ragged Rocks* 'But I'm *going* to get it published,' he declared to one of them. 'My first hero was P.G. Wodehouse and he said you learn from seeing your own rubbish in print.'

Still, it was not until twenty years later that he was finally goaded into writing his memoirs. Just prior to this he had started to tease journalists interviewing him. 'Of course, you really want the dirt on me,' he would grin. 'But I won't tell you because I intend to spill it all myself. In a book.'

Niv's two autobiographical books about life in Hollywood are full of stories about his friends. But it is a remarkable fact that he lost not a single one of them through anything he said: a rare occurrence indeed where show-business 'memoirs' are usually concerned. He was, though, typically deprecating of his literary skill. 'I'm not a writer,' he said in 1977 after the publication of *Bring On the Empty Horses*. 'I've just had two accidental successes.'

The reason for these 'accidental successes', David believed, was his memory and being honest in everything he wrote. 'Dishonesty must be the worst crime,' he said in 1979. 'Oh, you embroider a good story to make it sound funnier. That's different. You're not harming anyone. But I think you should always think twice before saying anything in case it hurts another person unnecessarily. It's so easy to wound someone without realising it.'

Both books are also typical of Niv in that most of the jokes he tells are against *himself*: there is no self-consciousness and a complete lack of concern about his own dignity. These facts endeared him even more to a public that already admired him for his work in films and television. Indeed, the success of these works caused one reviewer to proffer the opinion that David Niven might ultimately be remembered more for his writing than his acting!

Overleaf: David Niven, devoted husband and father, with his wife, Hjordis.

19

David Niven — toast of the publishing world in April 1973.

Which brings me neatly to the point of this book. For the reader might well ask if Niv has not already told us everything about himself in his own words? Hadn't he even informed one journalist in 1977 pressing him about more memoirs that he had 'scraped the barrel' of his anecdotes? Indeed that *is* what he said. But I have been something of a collector of Niven stories for many years, and I know that not all of those he told found their way into the pages of those two books. Not, let me hasten to add, because they were too mischievous or crude (though David *could* tell such tales if he wanted to!), but doubtless because even with his remarkable powers of recall and excellent press cuttings files, there were still some that got overlooked. And it is these which I have gathered in the pages which follow. I believe that they form a neat postscript – not to say an embellishment – to what he has already told us in *The Moon's a Balloon* and *Bring On the Empty Horses*.

David was widely admired by his fellow professionals in the film business and many of his closest friends came from their ranks. These were his 'chums', as he liked to call them. They, and the others who became his intimates from the worlds of literature, the law and even politics, felt an overwhelming sense of loss at his death and readily responded to my suggestion that they might like to pay tribute to him in this book. Their contributions, most of them containing the kind of anecdotes about Niv that he himself delighted in telling, form another important section.

To these two sections I have added a complete filmography of his screen appearances, and also discovered one of his long forgotten articles about Hollywood written in 1946 and here reprinted for the very first time. I trust his shade will not blanch at anything I or my contributors have written – though I suspect a good deal of it would give him a wry smile or even a good laugh! I am afraid, though, that I cannot oblige him in one request he made to several journalists over the years. 'Write something nasty about me,' he would entreat them, 'it will teach me a lesson.' None ever did, for there were no grounds to do so – and nor can I.

Niv knew how he would like to be remembered. 'For having gone through life without leaving any shambles behind, for behaving reasonably well, for not having done anything really awful to anyone, for having been fairly honest. And for having a good time.' All that he achieved in good measure, and we are all the poorer for his passing. I do not think any of us will ever forget that remarkable face – 'like two pounds of halibut and an explosion in an old clothes cupboard' was how he once described it! – or that irresistible smile that could light up a room the moment he walked into it. Nor will we forget how he plucked stories from that raconteur's grab-bag which was his extraordinary mind. If Niv knew one thing from his lifetime of experience it was how to *entertain* on the screen, in print and in person.

That might, in fact, serve very well as his epitaph. But, typically, Niv had already decided what he wanted inscribed on his tombstone, and in the four words he picked was encapsulated perhaps the one reason above all others why he was so widely loved and admired. The words were:

HE TRIED IT ALL.

Peter Haining
December, 1983

'Anglo-Saxon Type 2008' — an early Hollywood publicity photograph.

Anglo-Saxon Type 2008

The Life and Uproarious Times of Our Hero

To HIS millions of admirers David Niven was – apart from being the archetypal gentleman in life as well as on screen – also, apparently, a typical Scotsman: canny in his dealings, possessing a dry sense of humour and having a healthy regard for money. Indeed, there is not a single biography of him – not even *The Times* obituary or his own hugely successful autobiography – that indicate anything other than that he was born in Scotland, at Kirriemuir, on 1 March 1910. It is a statement that has remained unchallenged for half a century since first published when David entered film business in the thirties, and has, naturally, given the small Highland town not far from Dundee, cause to claim him its most famous son, second only to the great author, J.M. Barrie. (And how suitable that Niven, the ageless charmer, should be linked with the man who gave the world Peter Pan?)

Yet the truth of the matter is that James David Graham Niven, as he was christened, actually first saw the light of day in London – in the very heart of the area whose residents he was later to typify so often on the screen: Belgravia. For as his birth certificate reproduced here quite clearly shows, the youngest of William Niven's four children was born in Belgrave Mansions, an imposing block of typical London town houses in Grosvenor Gardens, just round the corner from Buckingham Palace Road and Victoria Station. The building was evidently his parents' town residence at a time when their fortunes were buoyant.

Although it still survives today, the block is now taken up by flats and business offices. New, too, from the days when the youngest Niven arrived is the statue of Field Marshal Foch (1851–1929) standing on the small triangle of greensward which faces the former Belgrave Mansions. It is somehow appropriate that this remarkable French hero of World War I should be in the square where Niven was born: for his mother was a Frenchwoman and his father was to fall as a casualty of that self-same war. David's father was William Edward Graham Niven, a blond-haired, handsome man who described himself as a 'landed proprietor' of Carswell Manor in Faringdon, Berkshire, while his mother was a dark, beautiful lady called Henrietta Julia Niven (formerly de Gacher). The couple had met and fallen in love in France and raised five children, two girls Joyce and Grizel, and two boys, Henri, (known as Max), and David

David has, of course, written in his autobiography of his somewhat feckless father and how little he got to know of him in the five years before his death in 1915. Niven senior had joined the Berkshire Yeomanry and was serving as a lieutenant when he took part in the landing on the Gallipoli Peninsula and was killed by withering Turkish gunfire on 21 August. He was just twenty-five years old.

Long before writing his book, Niv had this to say of his father back in 1957: 'He was what is laughingly referred to as a gentleman of leisure. He was very well endowed but he spent the lot. He adored his spree and gave everyone a wonderful time. When I appeared on the scene we lived mostly in Scotland in a large country house staffed with footmen, butlers and gamekeepers. We also had a tame bookmaker (or so my father thought). My father devoted hours to the scientific study of thoroughbred horses, but he must have been reading the wrong reference books. By the time I was two years old he was bust: the horses had the rest of our money and we had to give up the large country house.

'When the First World War started he joined the Army and was killed at the Dardanelles. I do not remember much about him. He was only twenty-five, and he got nothing in exchange for his life except a sense of loss and a nostalgic affection from four children who barely knew him.'

Although William Niven never rose higher in the ranks than second lieutenant, when David reached Hollywood he was 'promoted' to a General by Sam Goldwyn's publicity department – the same department that also gave Niv's birthplace as Kirriemuir. Of such, of course, are legends made – but David himself was not strictly correct in implying that his father died penniless. For although he had certainly spent most of his inheritance, his will (which gave the family address as Golden Farm, Cirencester, Gloucestershire) declared that he left the quite considerable sum of £5,893 3s 10d.

26

David's mother, Henrietta, who he wrote was 'very beautiful, very musical, very sad and lived on cloud nine', kept the family together after the death of her husband, although it was not until much later in his life that Niv realised just what strain she must have been under. This understanding came in 1977 when his sister Grizel gave him a large box of old family letters.

'Several of these spoke of Lieutenant Niven as a fine leader and a marvellous man,' he said. 'It's pretty obvious that people adored him. But what I didn't know until reading the letters was that for two years no one knew he was dead. He was listed as "missing" and my mother was going mad. She didn't get condolences – a form letter – until the end of 1917. What I took for my mother's indifference was a nightmarish preoccupation – another Niven had come up on some POW list – and the awful strain of trying to keep the family together with no money.'

To support and educate her children, Mrs Niven had to sell the farm at Cirencester where they had also spent part of their youth. These were just two of several moves that David was later to recall. 'It was a real struggle for my mother,' he reflected, 'and you can trace the decline in the family fortunes by the lowering in tone of our different addresses. We went from Craig House in Kirriemuir to Fairford Park, Gloucestershire; Golden Farm, Cirencester to 47 Cadogan Place, London; 110 Sloane Street to 11 Cheyne Walk; and finally to Rose Cottage, Bembridge on the Isle of Wight. The cottage had actually been condemned by the local authorities and only our combined weight kept it fastened to the ground!'

Although David says in his book that his mother had several admirers – eventually marrying one in March 1919, Sir Thomas Comyn-Platt, a Conservative M.P. – he makes no elaboration of an earlier remark that Henrietta Julia Niven had a hankering after utilising her undoubted beauty to become a film star. 'She even got a job occasionally as a film extra,' he told an interviewer in 1957, 'which was something for a woman in those days.'

There are, unfortunately, no records that can be traced to substantiate this claim. Clearly, though, there was a desire in his mother to perform, and a taste for flamboyance in his father, which mingled in David to create his unique personality.

But despite all the disruption of his childhood, David formed a deep and abiding closeness to his older sister, Grizel, who remained a trusted confidante throughout his lifetime. He nicknamed her with that brand of humour which was to become such a trademark of his life as 'Gump', an 'in' word of the twenties for a lunatic! Speaking recently she said: 'We were always together as children. To some extent we were thrown together – me, the older sister, looking after the baby of the family. But there was far more to it than that. We even looked very like each other. While the rest of the family was dark and rather French in looks, David and I had the same shock of fair, unruly curls and bright blue eyes. We also had the same rebellious and sometimes shocking temperament. But he was even more uncontrollable than me. By the age of seven he was already established as the boss, and I had to learn to play cricket, sail, swim and even fight a bit.'

Grizel did, she says, manage to exert an influence on her younger brother when it came to looking for a job. She had by then gone into the theatre and encouraged him to try acting. Today, in her seventy-fifth year, she still lives in London, well-known as an accomplished artist.

Niv's schooldays at a succession of barbaric prep schools where he was despatched by his stepfather — who had taken an almost immediate dislike to him — were marked by his either absconding or being expelled. Nicknamed 'Podger' because, he says, he was a rather plump, round-faced boy, he was harshly treated by most of the masters and unmercifully bullied by older boys. As a result he turned to clowning to amuse those who might otherwise torment him, and in so doing learned for the first time of his inherent ability to entertain.

One incident which demonstrated this was recalled for me recently by the sculptor John Doubleday, creator of the statue of Charlie Chaplin in London's Leicester Square, who attended one of Niv's schools, Stowe, though some years after him, but found his name was already a by-word. John told me, 'Apparently during a chemistry lesson, Niven had surreptitiously emptied a glass of sulphuric acid and refilled it with a similarly-coloured solution. Then, at a suitable moment, he had stood up, unstoppered the bottle, and before the science master's horrified gaze had poured the contents into his mouth, clutched his throat and gasped, ''This is the end!'' The escapade earned him a thrashing, of course, but it immediately became a piece of Stowe folklore!'

Niv developed a respect for anyone who rebelled against conformity when they were young. In 1969, talking to Arthur Helliwell, he confessed to a real admiration for youngsters growing up in the permissive society with their long hair, protest marches, pot-smoking and free love. It was a confession in stark contrast to the suave and sophisticated figure he had long established himself to be: but at the same time revealed the unsparing honesty of his nature. 'If I was young today I would have been a shocking young raver,' he said. 'Absolutely no doubt about it. I would never have experimented with hard drugs, but I *might* have smoked pot. I would definitely have chased the girls. I'd have probably played in a group. I might even have had a go at flower power or whatever they call it. And I would certainly have had long hair. Nothing wrong with long hair, anyway, if it's clean. Let's face it, we were just as ghastly as any other young generation. I certainly sowed bigger wild oats than most youngsters,' he added.

The archetypal Scotsman – but in fact, David's birth certificate reveals he was born in London! (The still is from *Bonnie Prince Charlie*, 1948).

CERTIFIED COPY OF AN ENTRY OF BIRTH

GIVEN AT THE GENERAL REGISTER OFFICE, LONDON

Application Number 4 427

REGISTRATION DISTRICT St. George Hanover Square

1910. BIRTH in the Sub-district of Belgrave in the County of London

No.	When and where born	Name, if any	Sex	Name and surname of father	Name, surname and maiden surname of mother	Occupation of father	Signature, description and residence of informant	When registered	Signature of registrar	Name entered after registration
75.	First March 1910. Belgrave Mansions	James David Graham	Boy	William Edward Graham Niven Barnwell Manor Barkshire	Henrietta Julia Niven formerly de Gacher	Landed Proprietor	W.E. Graham Niven Father Barnwell Manor Farmgdon, Berkshire	Eighth April 1910.	J.C. Armstrong Registrar.	

CERTIFIED to be a true copy of an entry in the certified copy of a Register of Births in the District above mentioned.
Given at the GENERAL REGISTER OFFICE, LONDON, under the Seal of the said Office, the 26th day of September 1953

Niv admitted he got interested in drink very early in his life. 'Soon after my fourteenth birthday I was found face down in a rhododendron bush after finishing off half a bottle of brandy. But, thereafter, I learned to drink and to hold my drink like a gentleman, which was frightfully useful when I shared a beach house with Errol Flynn that we called "Cirrhosis-on-Sea".'

Smoking, though, was something he avoided. His mother offered him £50 to keep off cigarettes until he was eighteen. And, as he had already become something of an astute handler of money by this age, he offered to carry on until he was twenty-one for another £100! Thereafter, he said, he wasn't interested.

Girls were a very different matter. 'Sex?' he said. 'I was at it as soon as I knew what it was all about. I'd certainly lost my virginity by the time I was sixteen. And seduction was a wonderful sport in those days, with half a dozen petticoats to fight your way through! Can't be half as much fun for young men today with their birds in body stockings. Booze, birds and bookmakers have all played a part in my misspent life. I started young, I learned fast, and between the ages of fourteen and eighteen I was an absolute shocker. But no regrets – it was all lovely fun!'

One of the most famous stories from David's autobiography is, of course, his love affair with the pretty, honey-blonde, seventeen-year-old prostitute named Nessie 'with her voluptuous but somehow innocent body and legs that went on forever', whom he met in Piccadilly when he was just fourteen years old. She it was who introduced him to the joys of sex with a mixture of expertise and delightful Cockney wit which remained one of the most enduring memories of his youth. Indeed, few young men can have enjoyed such an extraordinary relationship at that age lasting for four years.

David disguised the identity of the young woman under the name of Nessie and, frankly, never expected to see or hear of her again when they finally parted in 1928 as he sailed off to Malta with the Highland Light Infantry. She had long before told him that her ambition was to 'marry some nice Yank or Canadian and fuck off abroad and 'ave kids.' A last letter which reached him in Malta confirmed that her wish had been granted. He was, though, devastated. 'When she walked out of my life I was heartbroken' he said later. 'She meant a great deal to me. I was really in love with her.'

But fate has a habit of playing a hand in the lives of people like David Niven and in 1973, while he was touring America to publicise *The Moon's a Balloon*, something quite extraordinary happened. During the course of a television interview with Dick Cavett he spoke again about his passionate relationship with Nessie. Immediately the studio telephones began to ring with callers claiming to be the long-lost Nessie. David himself explains what happened next. 'But I knew they weren't her, just jokers having a bit of fun,' he said. 'You see in my autobiography I'd written about how she had got married and gone off to Seattle with her husband. And that's what I discussed with Dick Cavett. But I *hadn't* revealed that her name wasn't really Nessie and that she'd gone to live in the American mid-west, not Seattle.'

But amongst all the piles of messages he spotted one that stopped him dead in his tracks. 'I just happened to catch sight of the telephone exchange and the name one of the callers had given, and my heart missed a beat. Because it was Nessie's name and it was from the town where I knew she had gone! My hand was shaking as I dialled that number. And it bloody well was her! She sounded marvellous, although she had lost her lovely Cockney voice. She had married an American businessman like she said she would. She told me she was very fat now. But I still had that image of her. A Twiggy-type. Except that Nessie had a great figure. I'd have loved to have seen her, of course I would. She wouldn't have minded really . . . but she said, "Better not". She was so sweet and so funny. She's still married, and a grandmother now with four grandchildren. And what's more she's the head of the Parent-Teacher Association. Can you imagine it? Isn't it funny how life turns out?'

To those who questioned how an international film star could admit to having had an affair with a prostitute, David gave his usual forthright answer. 'I certainly think it was unusual for a fourteen-year-old, however advanced, to have fallen in love with a whore, but I'm certainly not ashamed of anything I've done. That included.'

The years which spanned David's relationship with Nessie saw him change from a raw youth to a man, putting his schooldays behind him (with only the consolation of having developed his inclination for clowning by taking leading roles in several concerts, irresistibly drawn by 'the call of the greasepaint') and after an ill-fated interview to join the Navy at Dartmouth, arranged by his mother, finally entered Sandhurst Military College in order to become an Army officer. Nessie's influence – or perhaps her exertions – had in the meantime enabled David to lose much of his puppy fat as well as to take an interest in games, and he was now proficient in athletics, rugby, cricket, even fencing and boxing. He had grown up tall, straight-backed, well-built and undeniably handsome.

During his time at Sandhurst, David again appeared on stage in several concerts and also wrote a number of sketches for himself. He had also begun visiting London theatres and a chance meeting with a beautiful young actress named Ann Todd made him 'incurably stagestruck'. She, in turn, was to introduce him to another fast rising young actor named Laurence Olivier who was to become a lifelong friend and godfather to one of his children.

As the months passed, David became increasingly frustrated. But, he asked himself, what else had life to offer? 'It wasn't that I was in love with the Army,' he said years later with typical good humour. 'It was just the best thing we could think of to get a job. So I got on as best I could and by the

The young Niven
in the Highland
Light Infantry
when the Army
seemed destined
to be his career.

time I was eighteen I became a second lieutenant. I realised that at the end of eighteen years' service my creditors, if they were lucky, could address me as Captain Niven. And after another eighteen years I would be Major Niven, with twice as many bills.'

Because of his early Scottish associations, David felt he would like to be commissioned in the Argyll and Sutherland Highlanders, and in making his application to the War Office listed his preferred regiments, ending with the remark, 'Anything but the Highland Light Infantry'. Inevitably, of course, it was to the Highland Light Infantry he was sent – and almost immediately thereafter he was posted to Malta. He found the place had 'no trees, many sandflies, horrible smells and few girls'. This latter deprivation hit him particularly grievously, having just parted from the voluptuous Nessie after four passionate years.

'I am ashamed to say,' he wrote in 1958, 'that my stay on the island was one small calamity after another.'

It was, though, the place where he met the 'amazing and wondrous creature' Michael Trubshawe, an immensely tall moustached Englishman who, rather like Niv, had unexpectedly found himself in the Highland regiment. The two men formed an immediate friendship that remained undiminished until the day of David's death. Trubshawe, who himself became an actor after a period as a publican, was described by Niven in his autobiography as 'highly eccentric with a wild and woolly sense of the ridiculous . . . in short, an Elizabethan with a hunting horn.'

In Trubshawe's company – as *The Moon's a Balloon* has related in hilarious detail – it is no wonder 'Niv' staggered from one calamity to another.

'During one long hot spell,' he noted in 1958, 'a fellow officer, the inimitable Michael Trubshawe, and I rebelled against the heavy regulation steel helmets and sent to a London toyshop for two imitation ones made of *papier mâché*. Nothing was noticed until the third time we wore them. It was a dress parade, and then right in the middle there was a cloudburst. In next to no time the paper hats had drooped down over our eyes. We looked like two drunken gnomes at a pantomime with bluebells on our heads!

'Shortly after I was through being confined to quarters for that offence I was on the way to the parade ground in full uniform when I playfully thrust my officer's sword into a dummy used for bayonet practice. The blade snapped off about six inches from the hilt, leaving me with the crazy-looking dagger instead of a sword. There was no time to get another and presently, during the ritual, the adjutant called out, "Officers, draw your swords!" So I did. I must have looked pretty silly, standing there in front of the whole regiment with my midget-sized blade, and the adjutant said sarcastically, "Stick an olive on that, Niven, and I'll send for a martini." Away to confinement I went.

'I had no great talent for swordsmanship, but in spite of my Maltese fumblings I eventually learned how to handle a blade. This doubtful skill, coupled with a scientific knowledge of drinkable gin, also acquired at Malta, made my later Hollywood assignments much easier.

'I was on Malta for over three years and it was ghastly. I've never been so bored in my life and the Army got pretty sick of me, too. In one of his annual reports to the colonel, my commanding officer said, "In a few respects this officer is excellent, but after three years in Malta he knows less about the Army than the Navy." The parting of our ways was obviously not far off!'

Before David did actually quit the Army he had a brief trip to America at Christmas 1932 as the guest of the heiress Barbara Hutton whom he had earlier met while on leave from Malta in London. It was an unforgettable experience. 'The images of long ago are often warped by time,' he was to write twenty years later, 'and the colours seem brighter than they really were. But surely no young man ever entered paradise – as the United States seemed to me – with more wonder, or had to leave it with deeper regret.

'The montage of memory brings back many things about that first visit – a suite at the Pierre, the magic of Broadway or Fifth Avenue, sumptuous dinners at the Colony, or the Automat where I went on the few occasions when I had to entertain myself.'

Niv returned to England reluctantly and only an almost endless round of pranks with Trubshawe coupled with a lively social life prevented him resigning immediately. One of his friends, Priscilla Weigall, seemingly had an insight into where his future lay and informed him one day that he should be a movie actor – and promptly got him a day's work as an extra on a film being made at Sound City. However, his brief appearance in *All the Winners* was not such a success as to convince him then that that was where his future lay.

Another brush with the Army authorities in May 1933 precipitated a decision Niv knew was inevitable. His insubordination this time, he thought, could only lead to a court marshall and probably public disgrace, so he hastily sat down and rather less than formally tendered his resignation to his Colonel Alec Telfer-Smollett:

> *Dear Colonel,*
>   Request permission to resign commission.
>
>   *Love,*
>   *Niven*

Without waiting for a reply, David swiftly raised the fare for a return trip back across the Atlantic and before the end of the month was once more in North America. His early adventures in Canada and America when he was 'broke and often hungry' form one of the most enjoyable sections of his autobiography, although there are at least a couple of stories from this period which he did not record. With America in the grip of the Depression, he found work extremely hard to come by and among his temporary jobs was selling liquor – then just coming back on public sale after the repeal of the Prohibition Laws.

His employment with 'Twenty-One Club Selected Stores Ltd' was to prove just as disastrous as his life in the Army had done. 'I took a telephone order from one of the lusher night spots in Manhattan for fifty cases of champagne,' he recalled in 1953. 'I pulled up in a truck outside the place and several white-coated characters appeared, unloaded the cases on the sidewalk, and handed me a cheque. I drove happily away. It wasn't until an hour later that I learned that no sooner had our truck moved off than another pulled up in the same spot, the cases were loaded aboard – and never seen again by my clients! And, of course, the cheque bounced. It was as smooth a highjack as Manhattan had seen in weeks, and five minutes after the firm had got the picture clear I was out on the sidewalk again – job hunting.'

Perhaps even more amusing was his attempt to promote pony racing. 'It was while I was in New York that I encountered a most remarkable promoter named Douglas Hertz and between us we dreamed up an organisation called *The American Pony Express Racing Association*. The idea was to set up teams of polo ponies and have indoor races on small tracks in large auditoriums. We decided on polo ponies because running counter-clockwise they could easily handle the short turns as they went round and round.

'We sold stock to the sporting minded with a taste for the bizarre – the late Damon Runyon was among the enthusiastic investors – and used the money to buy more than 100 broken-down and slightly neurotic ponies, with genuine but equally neurotic Indians and cowboys as jockeys.

'Opening night in the Municipal Auditorium at Atlantic City was a sell-out. I recall with a guilty shudder that I led the grand march billed as Captain David Niven of the Royal North West Mounted Police.'

Although the event was an undoubted success, Niven and his partner attracted the attention of some underworld characters who felt they should have a cut of the profits. When the promoters refused, the show was rapidly sabotaged. In three days they were closed down: Douglas Hertz left for the west coast and Niv, having sold the polo ponies, also hastily departed.

That, as far as *The Moon's a Balloon* is concerned, is the end of the story. But in fact there was a sequel which David revealed almost thirty years later.

'I was reminded of the Pony Racing Association in 1938 after I had made *Bachelor Mother* with Ginger Rogers,' he said. 'At a party to celebrate the completion of the picture, I was suddenly tapped on the shoulder by a guest.

'You David Niven?' the man asked.

'Yes,' I said.

'*The* David Niven?'

'Why, yes,' I said preening a little. 'I suppose you could call me that.'

'Well' – he took a deep breath, and by now all the guests were staring at us – 'I think everybody in this room ought to know you're a crook.'

'Who me?' I said, wishing he wouldn't talk so loud.

'Yes you!' he snapped. 'Four years ago you sold me ten so-called polo ponies.'

'Ah,' I said quickly, 'fine animals.'

'Like hell they were!' he said. 'I had to give them away because they would only turn left!'

There followed some further well-documented adventures in Bermuda and Cuba before David arrived in Hollywood in 1934. Once again, polo ponies featured in his life. By now he was well practised in the art of the farcical and he was unable to resist the temptation to feed a local reporter a story that he was a wealthy sportsman with special plans for his future in the area. The following days the *Los Angeles Examiner* carried a photograph of him bearing the caption 'British Sportsman Arrives – Plans To Buy Over A Hundred Head of Polo Ponies.' In fact, he had no intention of going anywhere near polo ponies again (although he was to be unwittingly drawn into the hilarious polo match with Darryl Zanuck, the head of 20th Century-Fox, which is so uproariously told in his autobiography) and instead was bent on trying his luck as a film extra.

To this end he presented himself at Central Casting Office in Hollywood, from which all extras were drawn each day, and despite the discouraging notice outside the building, was registered as 'Anglo Saxon Type Number 2008'. He was, though, under no illusions about what lay ahead. 'It was sheer bloody conceit that had led me to believe I could act at all,' he recalled in 1976. 'I had done some acting at school, of course, and appeared in an Army concert once which brought the house down, and just because my mates responded somewhat enthusiastically to my shenanigans I believed that Hollywood would react in exactly the same way. Well, of course, it didn't. But I wasn't going to be defeated. So I took whatever work was going – even if it was only as an extra. And let me tell you that being an extra in the early thirties was no fun at all. You were paid a lousy two dollars and fifty cents a day – and your day began at five a.m.

'I can remember getting up at four in the morning, and, because I didn't have a car, I had to wait for an early bus to take me to the location where they were filming. Then, when I got there, I'd be painted yellow if I was required to be Chinese, or black if they wanted Negroes. More often than not it would rain – the day's shooting would be cancelled and I'd have to make my own way back to Hollywood, sopping wet, covered in filthy paint and minus my two dollars and fifty cents because in those days, when shooting was cancelled, the extras were never paid.

'It was quite common for us to be appearing in several films at the same time – even on the same day. We would all dash from one stage to the next and try to remember which costume we were supposed to be wearing. I did a lot of Westerns.

'One day only fourteen "extras" turned up for a crowd scene. The director went mad. He phoned the producer, who told him there was no budget to hire any more. "Just pretend it's a sleepy town" he said. That must have been the smallest town in Western history. We all spread ourselves out to make us look more, and just stood round pretending to pick our nails with pieces of wood!'

The reason David found himself playing in so many Westerns, he believed, was because he looked slightly sinister and could also ride a horse. This brought him within a whisker – perhaps a rather insubstantial whisker – of being cast as the original Hopalong Cassidy, the part that made William Boyd world-famous, according to another story that did not find a place in his autobiography. He recalled the events in July 1953.

'I was frequently cast as sinister Mexican peons, the kind of character who has a drooping moustache, peers out from under a large sombrero, and lurks outside the Lucky Chance Saloon whittling a stick and knifing the hero. For days I loitered round the lot, muttering "Caramba!", "Mama Mia!" and "Olé!" in a conscientious effort to get under the skin of the parts. To my intense relief no one thought me particularly odd. Indeed, as time passed, I found myself playing in Western after Western – twenty-seven in all.

'I was knocked down in bar-room brawls, shot-up by Texas Rangers and ridden over by sheriffs' posses. It was a wonderful experience, and even today I'm filled with nostalgia whenever I see a film with blazing 45s and the hero pressing his prairie rose to his chest.

'Of course, I never got to that stage myself. Although I played every other part, except the horse, in horse opera. I remained strictly a general utility man. Who was that shifty-looking barman, signalling furtively to the villain behind the hero's unsuspecting back? Why, Niven! And that drowsy cowhand guarding the sleeping herd as he nods over a dying fire? Me again. In the tiny world of the sagebush saga, I displayed a wild versatility.

'It was around this time I went after the role of Hopalong Cassidy. I had heard that there was an outfit planning a series of Westerns around a permanent central character. So I went along to the producer's office trying

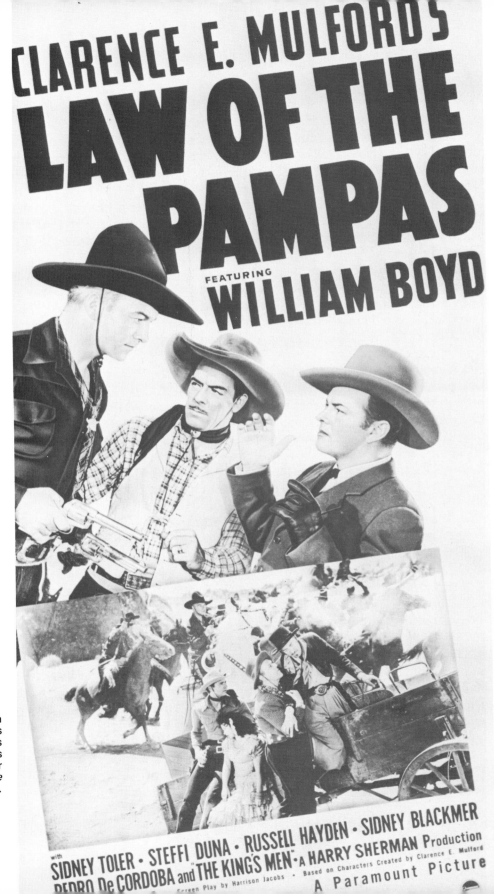

Niv the Western 'extra'! David has been identified as one of the extras on this poster for *Law of the Pampas* (1935).

to look bow-legged as though I'd been reared in the saddle.

'The man gave me a long, critical stare. "And what part of the great outdoors do you come from, son?" he said. Feeling a bit of a fraud, I mumbled, "London".

' "London, eh? Oh, you mean that cow-town in eastern Ontario? There's mighty nice cattle country in that part of Canada, I'm told."

'I felt I had to come clean, so I interrupted. "Er – well, actually I come from the other London – the one in Great Britain . . ."

'There was one of those difficult pauses. Then, his cigar quivering with emotion, he pointed firmly towards the door, and I made a hasty exit.

'Of course, Bill Boyd later made himself almost a legendary name out of those films. But I still wonder how *I* would have made out as old cowboy Niven!'

It was, of course, as the result of another part that he didn't get which gave 'old cowboy Niven' his real break into films: a chance remark by Irving Thalberg of MGM that he was thinking – only thinking – of signing David to a role in his forthcoming epic, *Mutiny on the Bounty*. Word of this got around Hollywood and almost before he knew what had happened, Niv had been snapped-up by Hollywood's legendary independent producer and gatherer of stars, Samuel Goldwyn. It was only later that David learned that all Thalberg had in mind for him was another 'extra' role – as one of the non-speaking English mutineers!

But with a seven-year contract, David, now twenty-six years old, had breached the portals of Hollywood and although his career was to be a chequered one mixed with good films and bad, as Goldwyn loaned him to one film company after another to learn his craft, he had cause ever after to be grateful to the man. Even the terrible feuds between them and the unhappy parting were to count as nothing in Niv's final assessment.

Reminiscing about Goldwyn in 1958 after he had won his Oscar for *Separate Tables* (made by rivals United Artists) he said, 'I don't know if Samuel Goldwyn ever believed the gossip about *Mutiny on the Bounty*. Perhaps he didn't. Perhaps he liked me and saw something that had escaped the others. But the fact remains that he did call me, and in a matter of hours I was shakily signing my name to a contract. My magnificent salary averaged about $65 a week, but it looked like a million to me, and it opened the doors to a whole new wonderful world.

'Over the years, much has been written about my feuds with Goldwyn. It is true that I was once bitter about the fact that he loaned me out to other studios for vast sums and compelled me to make films that curdled my soul – such as a series of dreary costume pictures with Alexander Korda or a co-starring mishmash with Shirley Temple.

'To me Goldwyn then was in a tight little empire. He could not have been anything else, I guess. Film-making was not a pattycake kind of game, and the competition was savage. On the other hand – and for this I am eternally grateful – Goldwyn transformed me from a hopeless amateur into a pro. He brought one dream to reality for instance, when he made it possible for me to co-star with my dear friend and helper Loretta Young in *Eternally Yours*. Thereafter I made many others with Loretta, including *The Bishop's Wife* and *The Perfect Marriage*.

'Fortunately, Goldwyn also lent me to David Selznick for *The Prisoner of Zenda*, to Warner Bros for *The Charge of the Light Brigade*, and to RKO for *Bachelor Mother* with Ginger Rogers. And, with Eddie Goulding's urging, he farmed me out to Warner's for *Dawn Patrol*, the picture that graduated me into the major leagues.

'In his way – and his fabulous record reflects it – Goldwyn is a genius. If he phoned me tomorrow and asked me to do a picture for him, I would come running.'

It is gratifying to be able to record that Goldwyn and Niven met again for the first time in eight years after the Oscar ceremony and despite their differences, it transpired that it was not only Niv who had retained fond memories of their association. At the time of his signing his contract, David had also started to make friends with a number of other British subjects who were resident in Hollywood, and cashing in on the fact that Film City was then going through something of a 'British Period' with the films it was making such as *David Copperfield, Disraeli, Sherlock Holmes* and so on. To this colony of expatriates belonged such stars as Cary Grant, Ronald Colman, Nigel Bruce, Ernest Torrance, Basil Rathbone, Herbert Marshall and C. Aubrey Smith, the doyen of them all, and organiser of the famous Hollywood Cricket Club. Niv was a delighted recruit to their ranks.

However, the most famous friendship of these years was to be with another 'expat' – but not an Englishman: the 'wild colonial boy', Australian Errol Flynn. So much has already been written about Flynn, the great film swashbuckler, his legendary sexual prowess and indulgence in drink and drugs, that a recap here is scarcely necessary. Yet for all his wildness, his unreliability and obvious ego, he was a man who left his mark on screen history and whose memory is still widely revered today. To the end of his days, David, too, retained a deep affection for the man he once referred to as 'a lovely maniac'.

'Errol Flynn is still the finest example of a rampant male that I've ever known,' he wrote some years after his friend's death in 1959. 'Outrageously handsome, he drove women absolutely crazy; and for him, the supply was endless.' David also said of Errol, 'the one thing about him was that you always knew exactly where you were with him because he would always let you down,' he equally felt 'a great friendship and compassion' and defended

On the set of *The Charge of the Light Brigade* (1936). A rare photograph of Niv with Errol Flynn and Michael Curtiz, the director who gave him the title for his second bestselling volume of autobiography.

Flynn vigorously against some of the extraordinary charges which were levelled against him after his death.

The two men first met in 1935 when Flynn was making what was to prove his first big hit *Captain Blood*, and David was trying to get his foot on the bottom rung of the ladder to stardom. Their friendship really blossomed shortly afterwards when they were cast in Warner Bros' *The Charge of the Light Brigade* – as Niv has described in his autobiography. Indeed, they set up bachelor quarters together in a house in North Linden Drive, Beverly Hills soon known as 'Cirrhosis-on-Sea' as they rapidly gained a reputation as the biggest hell-raisers and boozers around. The house was, as David later said, 'a hot bed of fun and bad behaviour'.

Off the Cuff: Errol Flynn, busy being "The Perfect Specimen" at Warners, is batching with David Niven. . . . Look at this for a list of Irishmen in "Submarine D I"—Pat O'Brien, George Brent, Frank McHugh, Reagan, O'Neil,

Another rare still of Niv and Errol Flynn while they were making *Dawn Patrol* in September 1937. Off-screen, the two men were also sharing the same house, as this early news clipping from *Movie Maker* reveals . . .

Overleaf: Niv learning about the joys of parenthood with Ginger Rogers in *Bachelor Mother* (1939). She, too, was to become a firm friend.

Their friendship spanned the years of World War II when David, of course, returned to England and served with the Army. Yet, despite their lack of contact during this time, he was totally convinced of the falseness of the most outrageous allegations subsequently published about Flynn: that he was a secret Nazi supporter and German agent. These charges were made public in 1980 by author Charles Higham, and instantly repudiated not only by Flynn's surviving family but also his friends and former associates. Foremost among these was David who said in February 1980: 'I knew him well before and after the war and he never showed any Nazi sympathies. Everyone in those days knew someone who knew someone who supported the Nazis. Obviously there was support for the Nazi cause. Otherwise they wouldn't have been able to annihilate six million Jews. But just because Errol knew someone – that doesn't make him a Nazi. If he had been alive today he would have got the biggest laugh out of reading suggestions he spied for Hitler.'

The truth of this matter does, though, make for interesting reading. For according to Charles Foster, a Canadian writer who for some years was Flynn's press secretary, the actor *did* provide information for the

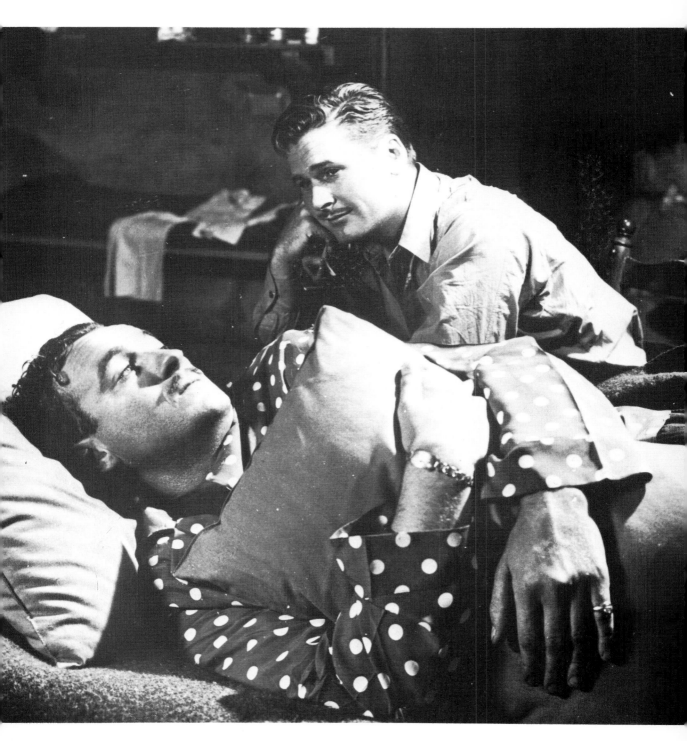

Germans – but it was all false and he was working under instructions from the American Government. Said Foster, 'I was a close friend of Flynn's during his final years, and only I, some high-placed officials in the U.S. Government and his friend the actor David Niven know the true story of Flynn's espionage work. The truth is, Flynn was operating under orders of the U.S. Government and feeding false information to German agents.

'He told me about his Second World War undercover activities in 1956 when we were attending a film festival in Berlin. He said he had a number of German friends in Hollywood. He liked the Germans as people, enjoyed the European lifestyle and frequently complained about Jewish movie moguls because they did not pay enough.

'Jack Warner also told me how he and Flynn fought like cats and dogs over money, but they were friends and often visited each other at their homes. But because Flynn would call Jews names, his German friends thought they had a sympathiser who would be willing to provide them with information. But when Flynn realised he was being pumped for information he went to the U.S. Government, told Intelligence officials what was happening, and they knew they had a link with German espionage operations. "You tell us what questions you're being asked, and we'll tell you what to reply," they told him,' added Foster.

This was the basis on which the accusation that Flynn had been a Nazi spy was mistakenly built, said Foster, also pointing out that the FBI had a number of reports which had been compiled about Flynn as well as various other foreign actors working in Hollywood at this time. The dossier on Flynn had been compiled on the personal instructions of the Director of the FBI, J. Edgar Hoover, he maintained. On this point, Niv himself was quick to comment. 'It's worth recalling,' he said, 'that J. Edgar Hoover was suspicious of everyone, even Adlai Stevenson!'

After *The Charge of the Light Brigade*, Niv made only one other picture with Flynn, in 1938, the widely acclaimed war story, *The Dawn Patrol*, also for Warner Bros. There had, though, been plans for the two men to be linked in *The Adventures of Robin Hood* which Errol filmed in 1937. David was earmarked for the role of Will Scarlet by Jack Warner himself, but Goldwyn had already loaned him to 20th Century-Fox for *Dinner at the Ritz* to be made at Denham Studios in England and that curtailed any such ideas.

Their friendship survived all the ups and downs of Flynn's wayward life, however – as David described at length in *Bring On the Empty Horses* – and according to a Los Angeles psychic, Damien Caldwell, Niv was conscious of Flynn's presence even long after the Australian actor had died. Caldwell said that he did frequent psychic readings for Niven. 'He had a strong belief in the after-life,' the psychic maintained in August 1983. 'David felt that Errol was a constant spiritual presence in his home. He felt Errol was often trying

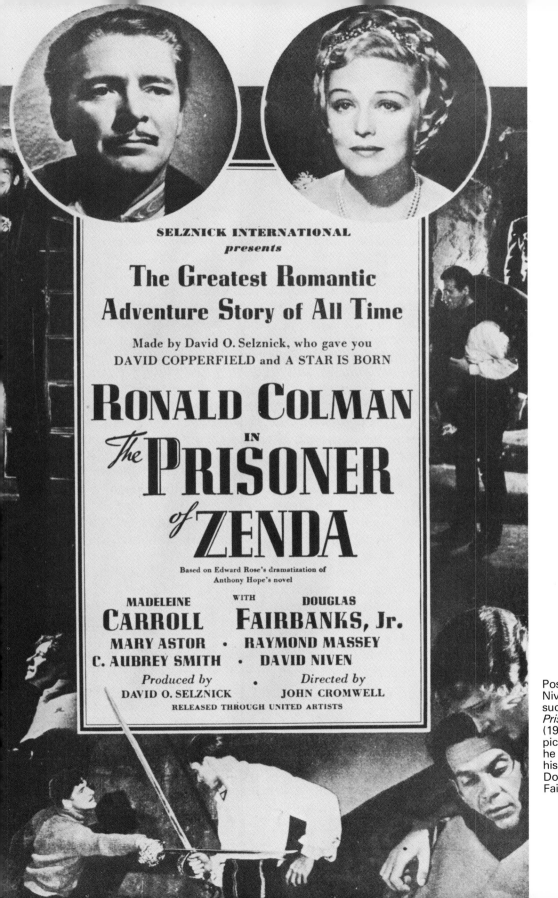

Poster for one of Niv's earliest successes, *The Prisoner of Zenda* (1937), the only picture in which he appeared with his lifelong friend, Douglas Fairbanks Jnr.

to save him from the craziness of Hollywood.

'David moved to Europe because he had a dream in which Errol told him to do so. He represented an era of Hollywood that had died and he never felt that he was part of the community again. But he was looking forward to a new spiritual life once he left this earth.'

After all the rumbustious fun of *The Charge of the Light Brigade*, Niv was pitched into another costume drama, *The Prisoner of Zenda*, in 1937 and formed another enduring though less volatile friendship with Douglas Fairbanks Jnr, whose famous father had welcomed him on his arrival in the film colony. Although this was to prove their only actual film together, Douglas and David never lost contact thereafter. For David, the picture also remained memorable because of a practical joke he played on his fellow actors. He recalled the incident in 1958.

'One of my early blood-and-thunder dramas was *The Prisoner of Zenda*, in which I was privileged to do heroics with Ronald Colman. During the indoor scenes I notices that all the extras were milling around a huge fruit-punch bowl. They looked unreal and vaguely unhappy, and I felt that some should at least frown or even quarrel to make the scene more lively.

'During a rest-period I went to Raymond Massey's dressing-room and swiped six bottles of gin. I carried the stuff out under my flowing cape, emptied it into the punch bowl, and stirred it with my sword. When the cast reassembled, I watched a couple of dead-pan extras gingerly sampling the now fortified fluid. They looked at each other wide-eyed, quickly dipped their pewter mugs for a refill, and then hotfooted around the set to spread the good news. Within thirty minutes the house cats turned into tigers. One extra took a poke at another, some burst into song, and one, filled with alcoholic daring, suddenly gave an inspired rendering of the soliloquy from *Hamlet*.

' "Craziest extras I ever had," director John Cromwell muttered. "What the devil's got into them?"

' "I think you really inspired them," I said.

' "Oh, really?" he said. He looked at me suspiciously for a moment, then went on with another take.'

David also had an amusing moment with another famous Hollywood director, Ernst Lubitsch, who directed his next picture, *Bluebeard's Eighth Wife* (1938) – although this time the laugh was on him. Niv thought Lubitsch 'a very funny little man'.

'He would squat on a ladder like a frog watching you go through a funny routine and he'd laugh so much he'd fall off. Then he'd get up and we'd go through the whole thing again with him still dying laughing – but giving a little advice here and there. By the tenth or twelfth take you realised you were far from your original interpretation – you were playing pure Lubitsch.'

The very first meeting years before between David and the director was also pure Lubitsch. It had occurred not long after Niv had first arrived in New York after leaving the Army. He had been invited to the home of Elsa Maxwell who informed him he should be in the movies. 'I'm serious,' she had told David. 'And I'm having Ernst Lubitsch to dinner on Wednesday night. Why don't you drop in after dinner and I'll introduce you?'

Niv takes up the story at this point: 'The great Lubitsch? What could I lose? I could have used a big steak as well, but I dropped in after dinner as Elsa suggested and just stood around. Lubitsch was there all right, and I shifted my stance from one foot to the other for a couple of hours and waited for the big moment. Presently, glancing at his watch and yawning, Lubitsch went past me, put on his coat, and disappeared. I crawled away quietly.

'Years later, when Lubitsch was casting *Bluebeard's Eighth Wife*, he gave me a very fine part in it, and I reminded him of the evening in the Maxwell apartment, and told him how unhappy I had been.

' ''Small world, David,'' he said. ''Now that you mention it, I can remember seeing you hovering in the background. I thought you were the butler!'' '

After being reunited with Errol Flynn in *The Dawn Patrol*, Niv at last found himself being cast in one of Sam Goldwyn's pictures. But what a role and what a picture! It was that of Edgar in *Wuthering Heights*, directed by William Wyler. Also in the line-up were two of the leading actors from his native England, Laurence Olivier and Flora Robson, as well as the accomplished Merle Oberon playing Cathy.

David had been longing for a really big break – and here it was. But he hated the part and he told Sam Goldwyn so. Goldwyn, though, was having none of it, and Niv was soon at work. In time he came to be grateful for that persuasion for the picture earned him critical acclaim and two more enduring friendships, with Laurence Olivier and Flora Robson. Not to mention another funny experience which he recounted in an article written in 1958.

'My big scene,' he recalled, 'came towards the end of the story when Cathy lies dead on her bed and Edgar, her husband, stands over her and, according to the script ''breaks down and sobs''. Merle Oberon was lying on the bed looking very gone when William Wyler called for silence.

' ''All right, David,'' he said, ''start crying.'' I screwed up my face, blinked my eyes and concentrated on sad things – the bills I couldn't pay, the beautiful girl who had dumped me for Errol Flynn, and so on, but it was no use.

' ''I'm sorry, Mr Wyler,'' I said. ''I can't cry. I've never been able to cry. Not even when I was a little boy.''

'They tried everything, but half an hour later I was still dry-eyed. Wyler, though, solved the crisis. He turned me away from the corpse and the camera focused on my back while I groaned, heaved my shoulders, and rocked back and forth.

'Months later, when *Wuthering Heights* was released, the critics were predicting a fine future for me, some saying, "Niven was superb . . . Most touching death-bed scene in years . . . Niven pulls at the heartstrings." No wonder, I thought, I love this business!'

As David was afterwards quick to confess, the success of this picture and its successor, *Bachelor Mother* made him begin to believe he was actually a star at last, and he became rather conceited. 'After all those tiny parts, I suddenly found myself one miraculous day billed "above the title", as they say, in a film called *Bachelor Mother* with Ginger Rogers. Well, my head expanded so much it practically became top heavy and was impossible to get a cardigan over. I was so darn conceited that do you know what I did? I went out, bought a camera and photographed all the billboards in Hollywood which carried posters of that particular film. At last I was a big star and I positively revelled in it. I honestly came to believe the publicity handouts they were writing about me. There was even a time when I was convinced I'd won the war single-handed – and, of course, not long after the war I got my come-uppance.

'Although I was hardly in demand when I returned to Hollywood, I was as cocky as hell – and told Sam Goldwyn that he didn't know how to run my career! Well, that bit of information didn't go down at all well. As a punishment I was loaned out to another studio to play a heavy in a dreadful Shirley Temple film *A Kiss for Corliss* (1949). Shortly after that I parted from Goldwyn. But there was no question about it. My behaviour was quite appalling.

'I suppose one of the most important things I learned in Hollywood all those years ago, was that only the second-raters allowed success to go to their heads. The giants of the industry – men like Gable and Jimmy Stewart, Bogart, the incomparable Fred Astaire, Ronnie Colman and Spencer Tracy all remained level-headed about their careers.'

The bust-up with Goldwyn was, however, some way in the future in the autumn of 1939 when the storm clouds gathering over Europe became unmistakable even to Niv riding his own personal Cloud Number Nine. After completing *Raffles*, a part which was tailor-made for him and with which he has remained identified, David felt an overwhelming urge to return home. He might have come to America to make his fortune, but a part of his heart still remained in England. And now England was faced with the Nazi menace. Niv wrote about his feelings at this time some years after the war was over.

As the 'Gentleman Cracksman' Raffles, in 1939, a part with which he became inextricably associated.

'In 1939,' he said, 'when the world was beginning to flame with war, and all my friends back in England were joining up, I knew I could not fight it out in Hollywood. I blew my savings on a monumental binge with Douglas

50

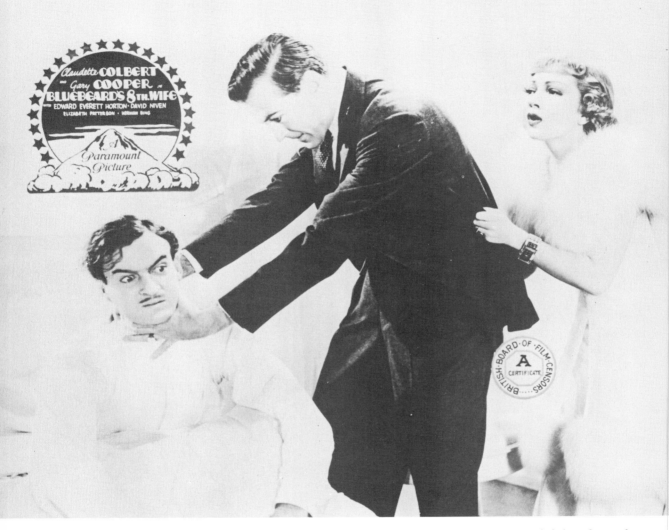

A rare still of David with two other early Hollywood friends, Claudette Colbert and Gary Cooper, taken in 1938.

Fairbanks Jnr, Robert Coote, Errol Flynn and other convivial pals and then, over Goldwyn's lamentations, booked a passage in an Italian ship to Britain.

'I had an uncanny feeling that I would never return, and so I wrote a rambling sentimental letter to Goldwyn. I told him of my gratitude and all the fine pictures we had made together and said goodbye for ever. Sam called me to his office the moment he received it, and Jock Lawrence, his publicity director, was there too.

' "David," Sam said, dabbing at his eyes "this is a very touching note. This letter is so private and personal that I want to leak it out to the press."

'By the time it leaked out, I had departed for what was probably the greatest adventure of my life. I got off to a bad start, unfortunately, because the studio drum beaters had made certain there would be flags waving on my return to London. It was embarrassing publicity for me, and I was not surprised when top-level officers in the RAF virtually accused me of wanting a little commercial glory.

' "We don't want any actors in the RAF," they said. "We already have plenty of good men."

'Having resigned my Regular commission five years before, I was not on the Reserve and there was certainly no rush for my services during the first weeks of the phony war. I went from office to office for weeks before I was accepted as a second lieutenant in the Rifle Brigade. I spent the next six years on active service in many zones of the European war, and hated every minute of it.'

Despite calling his war service 'probably the greatest adventure of my life', Niv remained reluctant to discuss this period of his life, and gave little away in either of his autobiographies. 'There are too many dead men looking over my shoulder,' he once said. Apart from a number of hilarious anecdotes; the fact that he was given leave to make two propaganda war films, playing a spitfire pilot in *The First of the Few* (1942) and a platoon commander in *The Way Ahead* (1944); that he rose from being a second lieutenant to lieutenant colonel serving in the commandos, General Montgomery's secret Phantom Reconnaissance Regiment; and that he saw action in Normandy, Holland, Belgium and Germany, this is the sum total of what he revealed of the next six-year period. Except, of course, that he had a brief stint in the War Office sharing a desk with a young captain destined for a hugely successful career in politics, Quintin Hogg, now Lord Hailsham, and for a time his batman was a young chap named Peter Ustinov!

Writer George Feifer was typical of many journalists who tried to pull the curtain back on Niv's wartime exploits, only to be told, 'I did my best, but it was never better than what I was told to do. Now that's enough of war.' But from his own enquiries Feifer was able to record in 1977, 'I have heard that his bravery was incontestable, his record distinguished. He was in the first Commando class in 1940 which took only the toughest specimens and trained them to exhaustion; and (as I discovered indirectly) he was seriously injured in the combat that otherwise engaged him almost continuously from D-Day to VE-Day.'

Undoubtedly, though, the most fascinating and least known part of his war service was on the fringe of Intelligence work, although quite how deeply involved he was it has proved impossible to discover. He certainly knew of the network of amateur spies known as 'Intrepid' based in Hollywood which had been set up by Sir William Stephenson, the Canadian director of Allied

Wartime Intelligence, in the years immediately prior to America's entry into the War. (It has, incidentally, also been suggested in another theory to explain Flynn's so-called spying, that he had come to the attention of the FBI because of enquiries he was making, or quiet services he was rendering, for Sir William Stephenson's network at this time.)

Taking direction from William Wyler on the set of *Wuthering Heights* in 1939. This picture was to provide two more lifelong friendships for Niv with a couple of other young actors from England, Laurence Olivier and Flora Robson.

In any event, Sir William has steadfastly refused to discuss his work — or those who worked for him — and only a detailed study of 'Intrepid' and the man who ran it, by a namesake, William Stevenson, which was turned into a television film in 1980 under the title, *A Man Called Intrepid*, lifted any of the secrecy surrounding the network. By a strange twist of fate, David was

The RAF refused to accept Niv when he applied to join up for War service – but he nonetheless gave a splendid performance as Wing Commander Geoffrey Crisp in *The First of the Few* (1942).

Below: Niv as Lt Jim Perry in *The Way Ahead* (1944) in which one of his co-stars, Peter Ustinov (*left*), also happened to be his off-screen batman!

As a far from ordinary naval officer, Lt Commander Finchhaven, in *The Extraordinary Seaman* (1968) rounding off Niv's portrayals of all three types of serviceman!

invited to play the part of Sir William Stephenson. He enjoyed the role enormously and was pressed into making a personal statement about 'Intrepid' while filming took place.

' "Intrepid" was an organisation so hush-hush that I actually worked alongside it as a British Intelligence office without realising,' he said. 'My operation, "Phantom", combined with "Intrepid" especially to secure the German Enigma coding machine, and we all know how much that contributed to our war effort by cracking their military ciphers.

'I know that Noël Coward, Leslie Howard and Ian Fleming were all involved in some way. I have heard that Gracie Fields was in there too, but the whole thing was fantastically secret. What amazes me is how so many showbusiness people could be involved in any kind of secret operation. We're famous for blurting out things, aren't we? Noël made a very unlikely-looking spy dressed in his red dinner jacket, but he was mixing with some very high-up people in France while doing shows for the troops. "Intrepid" was interested in any chance remarks made by important people. Perhaps they weren't of any use by themselves but put together with other remarks, they could give valuable information.'

It was also during the making of *A Man Called Intrepid* that Niv revealed that he was involved in a remarkable plot dreamed up by MI5 to fool the German High Command into believing that the Allied invasion of Europe would stem from North Africa – a story that was unknown for many years.

At the centre of this deception was to be a man impersonating General Montgomery, for it was believed if he was spotted in the Mediterranean by German spies – as he most certainly would be – the High Command back in Berlin would deduce that Monty was planning an invasion from that direction and not across the Channel as was actually proposed. David's part in this remarkable deception was to train the 'lookalike' Monty.

At first, though, MI5 asked *him* to play the role of the fake Montgomery! Although being attached to Montgomery's command he had seen the legendary General at close quarters, David knew he was not only much taller than Monty, but completely unlike him in appearance.

'Suddenly,' said David, 'I remembered having seen an older chap who was a lieutenant in the Pay Corps. He had been brilliantly mimicking Montgomery in a station show for the lads on Salisbury Plain. I told my MI5 interrogator that I thought he'd be pretty good at taking off Monty. And that was the end of the interview. That was the beginning and end of my secret mission. Or so I thought.

'Disappointed and unimpressed with my own impression of the whole affair, I went back to my unit. A little later I was grumpily told by my colonel that he didn't know what all this was about but I had been made deputy director of Army Kinematography. I made some sort of deprecating noise and he said, "It's only for a month. Go and get it done."

'So off I went to see this brigadier at Curzon Street House in Mayfair. He said: "What are you here for?" And I said: "I've been posted to you, Sir, as your deputy director," and he said: "But what are you going to *do*?" And I said: "I don't know, Sir," and he said: "Think up something for the troops. There's an office, go and write a film for the troops – something like that."

'Into this strange set-up there emerged Eric Ambler and a private called Peter Ustinov, who later became my batman.* After three weeks of racking my brains I came up with this fantastic idea of a morale-boosting film for the troops. It was Great Moments In Sport. Great goals, great Grand National winners and that sort of thing. I was just about to put pen to paper when in walked my original MI5 man. "We've located your man," he said, quite casually.

David Niven, the real-life wartime hero, portrayed not only Army officers on the screen, but also RAF and Navy personnel . . .

*Peter Ustinov was reunited with Niv in 1978 when they filmed *Death on the Nile* with Maggie Smith and Bette Davis. In November 1978 he told this story of their working relationship with Bette Davis. 'On the eve of our first scene with her,' said Ustinov, 'David and I decided to retire early and mug up on our lines. We thought it best to be word perfect next day because she is renowned to be a stickler on that score. Well, it was about 3.30 in the morning when I decided I'd got it right. In the morning, however, David and I were astonished when Bette couldn't remember her lines. "It's no good," she sighed, "I'm dead tired. I've been up half the night learning *my* lines because I was worried that I would get it wrong in front of you guys." '

'I was considerably appreciative of his casualness because I had no idea what he was talking about. Then he recalled the Monty mimic and told me they had located him in Derby and I was to go up there and on some pretext or other bring him down to London. *Under no circumstances was he to know why.* I still had absolutely no idea what this was all about, but the penny had dropped that I had been duped and was sitting here in this phony job waiting for the Intelligence boys' next reason to use me. So like a good boy, I went up to Derby and somehow inveigled this Pay Corps gentleman to come back to London "for a special assignment". Whereupon, at enormous cost to the War Office, I put him up at the fashionable Rubens Hotel.

'My MI5 man's instructions were clear: "Get him in your office and ask him this list of questions." He thrust a sheet of paper at me. Then he added ominously, like something out of a bad movie: "I'll be there . . ." He was too; hiding behind a blooming great screen which he had erected near my desk so he could hear the unfortunate Lt M.E. Clifton James answering my pre-set list of questions, the reason for which I did not understand. Then as though on cue in another bad movie, my MI5 man leapt from behind his screen, vigorously waving his official badge.

' "I'm from MI5," he proclaimed with stentorian authority. Whereupon the poor fellow I was interviewing practically burst into tears, which aided my predicament because if he hadn't, maybe I would have. Of course, I exaggerate when I say burst into tears. I think a frightful state is a better description. Well, he was gibbering, anyway.

'It transpired that unaware of the historic mantle that was to be placed on his theatrical shoulders, the poor fellow felt that MI5 had another, more sinister, interest in him. He had been long ensconced with a lady who was not his wife. But he had been drawing marriage allowance for her. For this he believed the great might of MI5 had been unleashed upon him.

'Clifton James went on to play his part like a hero indeed, particularly when you consider the added strain of rank and class of those days. He was to go on after the successful completion of his mission to write a book of his exploits, and even to appear both as himself and General Montgomery in the film *I Was Monty's Double*. That was my one and only assistance to MI5. But at the end of it my actor's training did not desert me. As a final gesture I made sure that Monty's Double got a hefty pay rise – an actor's rate for the job . . .'

Despite the strain of war service, David never forgot that he was an actor, and another story which found no place in his books is an amusing reminder of the fact. This other wartime revelation was made in 1958 and gives an intriguing insight into the concerned and thoughtful side of Niv's character so often hidden behind the light-hearted banter.

'Once or twice in a man's life,' he reminisced, 'there comes a time when he

60

thinks he is about to die. In such grim moments fear can be vanquished by a word from a loved one or by the strength of deep faith. I had such a moment on a bleak, wet day in the spring of 1945, towards the end of the war. We were going to cross the Rhine that morning, and even the optimists were afraid the casualties would be high.

'Most men who go to war feel that they will live, no matter how many others are killed. I had the opposite thought – and with a certain justification. For male Nivens have been knocked off with monotonous regularity in war after war and generation after generation.

'Now standing there, waiting and going over my equipment, I had time to think, and little scenes from the past took shape in my mind. I remembered a Christmas when Irving Thalberg and Norma Shearer took a liking to a young actor named David Niven and generously gave him a brand new car. I never told them I kept it in a garage because I couldn't afford to buy petrol, and that I soon had to sell it to eat and pay the rent.

'I remembered being ill in a cheap, one-room walk-up apartment, and having a nurse named Marlene Dietrich expertly cook dinner for me on a rusty, two-burner stove. And I could hear Sam Goldwyn's voice on the eve of my departure for the war in 1939 saying: "Don't worry, David: I'll tell Hitler to shoot around you."

'Now we were ready, and men were checking their guns. At that instant, like a courier from heaven itslef, a sergeant ran down the line distributing a last-minute load of mail that had just arrived. The timing of this mail delivery was probably fine psychology, for, as men ripped open envelopes from home, I could see shining eyes and shoulders straightening up a bit, and tears that broke the tightness in their throats. I was hungry for a letter myself, and the breathless sergeant finally came trotting along to me. "Here you are, colonel," he said thrusting an envelope into my hand. "Just this one?" I asked. "That's all. Sorry, sir."

'I tore it open and pulled out a single sheet. This is what I read:

Lieutenant Colonel David Niven,
Army Field Post Office
Allied Expeditionary Force.

Dear Sir,
This is to inform you that we have absorbed the Leland Hayward Agency, of which you were a client. Therefore we are now handling your business.

Sincerely yours,
MUSIC CORPORATION OF AMERICA

'I was cheered up considerably. The thought of death no longer chilled my heart. I was in safe hands. MCA had never lost a man, and they weren't going to lose one now!'

David's concern about his safety had, of course, a wider implication than for his own life, because back in September 1940 he had met a beautiful young WAAF officer named Primula Rollo, fallen in love, and promptly married her at Huish Church on the Wiltshire Downs with the indefatigable Trubshawe as best man. Although David has given an account of their meeting in *The Moon's a Balloon*, there is a different version he delighted in telling for several years, and I quote from a late fifties account.

'The first time I saw her she was in uniform in a London nightclub,' he said, 'and I tossed a bread roll at her. The second meeting occurred during the blitz and I was at the fighter station at Heston. The aerodrome was being heavily bombed, so I jumped into a slit trench and landed on a white Pekinese which promptly bit me in the behind. It was Primula's dog and we had quite a little argument about who attacked whom first. She was the cipher officer at the station, and said she outranked me. I disagreed and we compromised. We were married ten days later and we were supremely happy.

'Primmie, as I called her, was bombed out of two houses, and moved twenty-eight times during the war years. Our oldest son, David, began life during an air raid. Minutes after he was born a Nazi bomb struck the hospital and killed twelve children.

'David was so used to seeing semi-demolished buildings that when he finally came to California and saw a half-finished new house, he cried, "Look, daddy! Bombed!" Our second boy, Jamie, was also a war baby.'

In August 1945 Niv was demobbed at Olympia in London, collected his 'demob suit' and wrote in the centre's visitors' book, 'It was a pleasure (signed) David Niven, Civvy.' At five o'clock the next morning he was on a film set at Denham playing an RAF squadron leader in *A Matter of Life and Death*, for J. Arthur Rank. Sam Goldwyn had not wasted any time in getting him back to work! It proved a rewarding film for David to recommence his career and was later selected for the first Royal Command Performance.

Niv and Primmie also found time to take their much-delayed honeymoon – although baby David Jnr was by now five years old and Jamie was due in November. They stayed at the Ferry Boat Inn at Helford Passage near Falmouth, a spot immortalised by Cornish author, Daphne du Maurier in her novel, *Frenchman's Creek*. They were idyllic days, as David was later to tell London estate agent, Mr S. St John Hartnell, when he was endeavouring to sell the property in the spring of 1983. Considering the pain he was in, Niv's reply of 6 May from St Jean Cap Ferrat is poignant as well as typical of his generosity of spirit.

Niv with his first wife, Primmie, and their son, David Jnr.

62

HOW DAVID NIVEN WAS WELCOMED
BACK TO HOLLYWOOD

HOLLYWOOD ONCE-OVER BY W. H. MOORING

HOLLYWOOD: It was strangely appropriate that David Niven and Douglas Fairbanks, Jr., both were welcomed back by the Hollywood Press on the same day.

They were good friends before the war, and during the whole time each seemed to stand out as a symbol of his own native land. They both "got into it" as soon as they could and stayed in it until the whole job was done.

Each of them has much the same outlook: neither will talk about war, much less about his own part in it. On the screen it would be equally easy for one or the other to play the same part. David could get away with an American character and Doug could get away with a British one.

Edmund Goulding, who gave us a terrific "stag" party at the famous Romanoff night-club to welcome David home, says that as long as both the British and American publics acclaim with equal enthusiasm both David and Doug, there is no reason at all for serious differences of opinion among British and American interests.

"You don't applaud a fellow if for any reason of human chemistry you feel a dislike for him," said Goulding over cocktails.

"The fact that British and Americans all applaud both of these fellows proves there is a deep underlying unity of tastes and aspirations between the British and American peoples."

It's a neat theory. I couldn't imagine either David or Doug giving a second thought to it, however, which probably goes to help prove it, anyway.

When Sam Goldwyn gave his welcome luncheon for David, I sat opposite Loretta Young and Teresa Wright. Hal Wallis and Nigel Bruce were within earshot and we started to talk—Loretta and I—about the day Niven first arrived in Hollywood.

I happened to be the first English-man he met. In fact, I can say, literally, that I brought David to Hollywood.

He joined producer-director Frank Lloyd and me out at sea off Santa Catalina island.

We'd gone out to take newsreel shots of the old *Bounty* firing a salute in honour of H.M.S. *Norfolk,* which had just cruised down the coastline from Santa Barbara. David had got aboard there, for he had friends among the officers. Hitch-hiking to Hollywood by battleship is surely novel, but that's what David did.

He joined us on our launch, came ashore with us at San Pedro and rode with us in an M-G-M studio limousine to the INSIDE of M-G-M studios. Then he wanted to get to Loretta's home.

"Could you give me a lift without trouble?" he asked. Of course I could and would. David was about to hop into my car when along came Robert Montgomery. David had met him once at a New York party.

Bob was passing the Young house and I was not, so David went along with him.

"And," Loretta reminded us, "a week later he wanted to know just how one gets into movies." She told him, with perfect truth, that there is no way: you either do or do not and nobody ever knows quite how it's done.

The next day David went to dinner with the Youngs again. During the meal he quietly said "Gretch" (that is Loretta's real name), "I signed a contract with Sam Goldwyn this morning!"

"Gretch" nearly fell off her chair. Later he had a small part in one of her pictures.

Now it wouldn't be at all churlish to point out that she is going to star in HIS picture, because although they actually co-star in Hal Wallis's production, *The Perfect Marriage,* about to start at the Paramount studio, David will most likely steal all the publicity.

Not deliberately, of course, but because he cannot help stealing it.

The American Press is all steamed up about his return because, truth is, the American public holds him in higher esteem than any other British actor (with the possible exception of Ronnie Colman) who ever came to Hollywood.

You should have been at Goulding's stag party. Everybody was there. Except David.

He had flu and got ordered to bed at Nigel Bruce's house where he was a guest. Goulding got the telephone company to lay on a special wire and David spoke from his bed and heard our speeches to him.

Not one word was said about the war. He had fixed that all round the town before he set foot back here.

At the Goldwyn lunch he set his foot down on all hero talk when he told "just one war story . . . my first and my last." He related how he'd been asked by some American friends to search out the grave of their son near Bastogne.

"I found it where they indicated I would," said David, "but it was in the middle of 27,000 others and I said to myself 'here, Niven, are 27,000 reasons why you should keep your mouth shut.'" The story had a profound effect.

Then up got Sam, the story teller. Those Goldwynisms have been faked a lot in order to build up personal colour for the famous producer, but he does, in fact, "talk backwards" quite a bit.

Obviously perspiring over a written speech he could not read (not because of illiteracy, but nervousness) Goldwyn started to ad lib.

"I wish," he said, "that David would promise me one thing. I wish he would write a book. I know he does wish to discuss his army experiences, . . . he wrote some wonderful letters all through the war to a lot of people in Hollywood and I wish he'd publish them in a book!"

Everybody roared, and to this moment I'll bet Goldwyn doesn't know why.

David isn't likely to publish letters he sent to his friends, but he did "publish" a few flu germs and some of us went home from his welcome-back party with a passport to delirium.

Charles Boyer, Bob Montgomery, Franchot Tone, Pat O'Brien, Wayne Morris, Frank Morgan, Reginald Owen, Reginald Gardiner, Alan Mowbray, Douglas Fairbanks, Jr., Lewis Milestone, Sid Grauman of the famous Chinese Theatre, and yours truly, all got it within the week. I tell you the Niven charm really is infectious!

Douglas Fairbanks, Jr., welcomed home by R-K-O the same afternoon, told me over a cocktail that he will be out of the American Navy in February and will start right away on the R-K-O film based on the adventures of "Sinbad." That sounds like following in his famous father's footsteps, doesn't it?

He certainly looks a great deal like his dad, although he is still youthful and slender.

Mary Pickford, another reminder of Douglas Senior, came to the party. With very little make-up she still looks remarkably young. Not one feature of the doll-like face we knew on the screen in the early 'teens has gone.

Answers to mailbag: Joan Leslie and Susan Peters are not sisters. Reason you have seen nothing of Susan on the screen lately is that she was seriously injured in a gun accident a year ago, lay entirely paralysed for many months and only now is beginning to sit up.

She cannot walk yet but may make one film for M-G-M this year, in which she plays a girl in a wheelchair.

Her husband, Richard Quine, now out of the U.S. Coast Guard, is picking up his screen career with M-G-M at once.

Various suggestions for an actor to play Winston Churchill have been forwarded to the right quarters, but Warners doubtless will choose a well-known actor. . . . My bet is either Charles Laughton or Robert Morley.

It's true many coincidences mark the lives of Deanna Durbin and Judy Garland . . . latest is they both have reservations in the same hospital for the same date for their forthcoming babies.

Dorothy Lamour's baby (Jan. 8th) is a boy, Gloria de Haven (John Payne) has a daughter.

Robert Hutton, still under contract to Warners, co-stars with Joan Leslie in *Too Young To Know.* He is divorced and often escorts Lana Turner these days.

Big mystery about Bing Crosby is really no mystery at all. He overworked last year and was "run down," so took a rest and a routine hospital check-up. . . . Spent Christmas in New York while Dixie Lee (his wife) and the boys stayed at their California home.

Dixie, who last year took an accidental overdose of sleeping tablets and almost died, this year fell and hurt herself.

Domestic disturbances and an overtax of work due to so many business and professional enterprises have further strained Bing's health but he is not dangerously ill.

His radio sponsor is suing him because Bing wants to drop a weekly broadcast at £1,250 a time, and the sponsor wishes him to keep it up. Don't you wish you could take it on for him, even at half-price?

"It was Loretta Young who told David Niven how and how not to get into the movies"

'Forgive mode of reply,' he wrote by hand, 'but I am ill and have problems writing and dictating. End of June '45 I came back from Germany and with some leave, waiting to be demobbed, took my wife on a delayed honeymoon to the Ferry Boat Inn. (Married in Sept. '40)

'Had superb time! One day prawning, an oyster man rowed by. He stopped and opened a dozen which we ate waist deep in water! He had a large bottle of beer!

'The sides of the river had sections of the Mulberry floating harbours (which made the "D Day" Normandy Landings possible) parked by them.

'It was so beautiful down there and after six and a half years of war, the peace, gentleness and kindness of the Ferry Boat and its "Patron" and staff and locals was a real joy for us. I hope someone nice buys the Inn.

'God defend us from a hot shot developer.

> *'Love to all —*
> *David Niven'*

In 1946 Niv returned to Hollywood and despite a cordial welcome from Goldwyn, found himself immediately sent over to Paramount to be reunited once again with Loretta Young in *The Perfect Marriage*. He enjoyed working with her and again there are two uncollected stories from the picture which deserve a place here.

The first concerned a bedroom scene he had to play with Loretta. Because of the rigid controls on what was permissible on screen, director Lewis Allen had to film this sequence with the utmost care. But, as David was later to recall, they still ran into problems.

'We were both in bed,' he said, 'with breakfast trays across our legs. Not touching each other, you understand, and very correctly dressed in pyjamas and dressing gowns.

'All of a sudden, in the middle of the scene, this little man from the Hay's censorship office leaps up and shouts for us to stop. "This is not good enough," he says, "Niven must have one of his feet on the floor." You know what? I slipped a disc passing the butter!'

In another scene David was filmed on a treadmill with background scenery representing New York. 'The trouble was,' he recalled later, 'it was a street scene and the same signs and buildings kept going past all the time. I was dancing with Loretta, but the worst part was having to change sides. I kept having to skip behind her and go round to the other side to make it look as if I was dancing in front of her!'

On his return to Hollywood, Niv had also decided to capitalise on some of the amusing things that happened to him as well as putting his literary bent to use. He had always been an enthusiastic letter writer, and now made an

Though David's journalist friend W.H. 'Bill' Mooring welcomed him back to Hollywood enthusiastically in February 1946, tragedy lay just around the corner with the sudden death of Primmie.

With another friend, Loretta Young, in *The Perfect Marriage* (1946) when Niv had to keep his feet on the ground in a bedroom scene.

agreement to write articles about life in Hollywood for the *Express* newspaper in London. (A typical and now extremely rare example is reprinted in this book for the first time in almost forty years.) Unfortunately, as David confessed in *Bring On the Empty Horses*, 'after filing a few efforts I realised that I could not wear two hats – I could not keep my friends and at the same time disclose their innermost workings to several million readers, so I asked for and was given my release from the arrangement.'

Nevertheless, Niv had got the bug for commercial writing, although he could have no idea of the stunning literary success that awaited him. Indeed, when another opportunity presented him with the chance to write something more substantial, he was far from an overnight success. 'Even as a young actor I longed to be a writer,' he confessed in 1978. 'Once when Sam Goldwyn had me on suspension I was conceited enough to think I could write a novel. It was called *Round the Ragged Rocks* and was published in Britain by The Cresset Press in 1951. It sold about 28,000 copies over the years and has, thankfully, long been out of print. I have no intention of letting it be reprinted, either!'

The rarity of this novel has made it something of a collectors' item today, and the British Museum's sole copy has been marked 'missing-mislaid' since 1963. (Stolen, no doubt!) Interestingly, too, Niv is described in the B.M. Catalogue as a 'novelist' rather than a film star or entertainer!

Round the Ragged Rocks is actually a much funnier and more accomplished comic novel than Niv would have people believe. It is the story of a young officer in the British Army on the eve of demobilisation in 1945. He has no money, no prospects, no ambition and no compunction when it comes to seducing a good-looking girl. So he decides to try his luck as an actor in Hollywood.

On his way to film city he has a whole series of slapstick adventures including chaperoning a prize bulldog which has been purchased with an eye on the American canned dogfood market, an afternoon full of disasters at an American football match, and a fancy dress party which he attends dressed as a goat. Through a string of lucky accidents he finally becomes a Hollywood star, but then turns bloated, pompous and arrogant. Only by finding true love is he saved from a meaningless and empty life.

Because there are elements of this plot that will be instantly familiar to readers of Niv's two bestsellers, it was only natural that he was asked in 1977: is the story autobiographical? He was, as always, disarmingly frank: 'Of course a lot of it happened. In Hollywood I had this sudden, enormous success. I believed my studio's ludicrous publicity about me. I think I was saved from being a total shit by the war, really. And I don't even know about that. When I finally reached my regiment in wartime Britain, I remembered what I'd sacrificed in California, and I wept. ''Christ, what have I done?'' I whispered. ''Was my volunteering just another stunt for show?'' And I think it was, partly. I really do think that what pushed me along was an awful lot of showing-off bravado.'

Despite the fact that Niv drew on personal experience for *Round the Ragged Rocks* – the formula that worked so spectacularly well in his two later autobiographies – the reason for its comparative lack of success was evidently that he had not yet realised that his great talent was not as a novelist disguising facts as fiction, but as a raconteur recounting the extraordinary things that had happened to him in just the way they had occurred. Or, perhaps, with just a *little* embellishment.

There was not much success either for David in his working life in the forties as his relationship with Goldwyn deteriorated and he was put into a string of indifferent films.

Then there was an even greater personal tragedy when Primmie accidentally fell down some stairs and died as a result of head injuries. She had only joined him in Hollywood five weeks earlier and he had been looking to her for support in his career as well as raising their two young sons in as normal a family environment as might be possible in the unreal world of Hollywood. She was just twenty-five years old.

To try and relieve his pain, Niv threw himself into work, and in the autumn of 1947 was sent reluctantly back to England to make another costume spectacular for Sir Alexander Korda, *Bonnie Prince Charlie*. As Niv later remarked in *The Moon's a Balloon* the only thing spectacular about the film was its spectacular failure. 'It was,' he said, 'one of those huge, florid extravaganzas that reek of disaster from the start.' The script was in a constant state of revision and there were three changes of director during the nine months of shooting. Apart from the awfulness of the picture – confirmed when it was released – Niv's stay in Britain only left him with two pleasant memories.

The first was an encounter with an old theatrical actor he bumped into the morning after a rare bit of relaxation as a guest at the Stage Golfing Society annual dinner.

'Did you enjoy yourself, my boy?' the elderly thespian enquired.

'Yes, sir.'

'Do you play?'

'Quite a bit,' replied David. 'I've a handicap of five.'

'I'm not talking about golf!' the veteran exploded testily. 'Do you play? Do you act!'

The second experience occurred on the set of *Bonnie Prince Charlie* and within a matter of days had filled the gaping hole left in his life by the death of Primmie. Called back to re-shoot a scene he thought was finished, he was momentarily annoyed to find someone sitting in his chair. But one look at the tall, slim, auburn-haired woman with her uptilted nose and dancing, grey eyes, and he was lost. Ten days later he married Hjordis Tersmeden, a leading Swedish model, at Chelsea Registrar's Office with the redoubtable Trubshawe again his best man.

'It has been a source of wonder to me,' he wrote later that same year, 'that a man could be so fantastically lucky twice. Hjordis will be embarrassed by practically anything I say about her . . . so let it suffice that only a very special person could pick up the shattered and lost little family that was mine at that moment and weld it into the happy group it has become ever since she appeared on the scene.'

Later, the couple adopted two little girls, Fiona and Kristina, and though like all couples, the Nivens were to have their ups and downs, they remained devoted to one another. David, who delighted in referring to Hjordis with a grin as 'a mad Swedish lady' also loved telling friends of the gold disc she wore around her neck. On it was inscribed the words: 'I am always allergic to penicillin and sometimes allergic to my husband.'

Despite the troubles Niv was having with Sam Goldwyn which culminated in the movie mogul releasing him from his contract in 1949, he tried hard to see that his two sons were not spoiled by the trappings of show business. Early on, he instilled into them what he considered a very realistic attitude towards their father's profession. Whenever they were questioned about what he did, he told them they were to say, 'My father is a very bad actor, but he absolutely *loves* doing it!' He nicknamed his eldest son David, 'Slasher Green', after his admiration for the comedian Sid Field, and both boys soon proved to have some of their father's capacity for trouble, as the following story which Niv related in 1960 clearly shows. It is interesting, too, because of the insight it gives into David's attitude towards boarding schools – quite understandable considering his own unhappy experiences!

'We British,' he wrote, 'are the only race in the world who rip their children away from the bosom of the family at the age of seven or eight and send them away to the tender mercies of total strangers dressed up as schoolmasters. It may be that in this way we breed a race that is at its best in adversity, but to me it has always seemed a ghastly system. However, much as I disliked it, it did seem preferable to bringing up two little boys in the goldfish bowl, lotus-eating atmosphere of Hollywood, so off they went to boarding schools in England.

'Seven thousand miles of separation is a lot and it made us all very unhappy, but the real shock came in the middle of one night. Suddenly I sat bolt upright, with the perspiration cascading off me; I had realised a dreadful truth . . . to bring the boys home to California for their holidays would cost me, during their schooldays, a little over £22,000 in air travel alone!

'A week later they were back swimming happily in the goldfish bowl and

browsing contentedly on the lotus.

'The best day-school near our home in California was Roman Catholic. The boys were not Catholic, but they were received with open arms and set off each morning carrying their lunch pails containing sandwiches and a vacuum flask of milk. It so happened that I always took an identical lunch pail to the studio, the only difference being that the milk in my vacuum flask was heavily fortified with rum.

'The boys had only been a week at their new seat of learning when the inevitable happened, the Mother Superior of the school telephoned me at the studio.

' "There is something rather peculiar about your sons," she said. "They are tottering about the playground and one of them is trying to bite the drawing mistress in the knee."

'The worst of this saga was that I got their damned milk!'

The boys also displayed the same quick wit as their father. When several of David's films, including *The Moon is Blue* (1952), *The Little Hut* (1956) and *Happy Anniversary* (1959) ran into trouble with the Catholic Church and were proscribed on the weekly lists issued by the church, the boys would run home shouting at the tops of their voices, 'We're banned again, Dad!'

Niv despised Hollywood's 'professional fathers' – the actors who used their children to gain extra publicity – and did not like the boys being photographed. He was anxious that they were not made to feel in any way special or privileged. As was almost inevitable in Niv's life, this attitude had an unexpected repercussion. Once again Niv got a phone call from the harassed Mother Superior. It was the day for the school photograph, she said, and all the pupils were assembled. All except the two Niven boys, that is. They had locked themselves in the lavatories and were refusing to come out and pose until their father gave permission!

The boys took a great interest in the films David made, and often asked why he had taken a particular role, especially if they thought it unsuitable. 'Because,' their father would reply with a wry smile, 'I have just had a very rude letter from the bank.'

Although with the passage of time the Nivens could list some of the most famous stars in Hollywood as their friends and frequently had the likes of Frank Sinatra, Cary Grant, Liz Taylor and Grace Kelly as house guests, the couple worked hard to raise the boys as normal, sensible children. Niv particularly wanted them to keep a sense of proportion and was rewarded when they reported an experience at New York airport on their way home from England. When an airline official caught sight of their name, and naturally enough enquired if they were related to David Niven, the boys found themselves the centre of attention.

'The man went into a kind of trance,' David said later, 'and proceeded

kindly but very misguidedly to give them VIP treatment – a nice little private waiting-room with coffee and doughnuts, no hold-up with the passports or standing around in a nasty cold Customs shed with the common herd; all in all a performance guaranteed to undermine the stability of practically anybody.

'Fortunately, the old indoctrination paid off once more, because when they told me about it they said, "Thank heavens he had seen *Around the World in Eighty Days*; if he'd seen *Bonnie Prince Charlie* he'd have put us on a plane for Siberia!" '

After leaving Goldwyn, David worked hard at establishing himself as a stylish and accomplished actor during the sixties, and apart from the love of his family, was sustained by a group of devoted friends. This circle increased with the passing years, for both Niv and Hjordis were always anxious for new experiences, always ready to meet and make new 'chums'.

'I hate having the same bunch of chums and never changing them,' he admitted in 1965. 'It must be awful, all getting old together, decrepit together, and finally dying together. We have tons of changing chums.'

One of Niv's closest friends was the late Princess Grace of Monaco whom he had first known when she was just plain Grace Kelly in Hollywood. Later, when David bought his home in the South of France, the buildings of Monaco were visible across the bay and the Nivens and the Rainiers frequently spent time in each other's company.

David delighted in recounting how Princess Grace would ask him to order forty pounds of pork sausages for her from Fortnum and Mason in London whenever he was there. 'Just send the bangers care of The Palace, Monte Carlo, I'd tell the assistant,' he chuckled as he thought about the startled reaction of the person serving him!

'We also had a man who worked for us called Barnado,' David would say, relating another Princess Grace story. 'He did everything. Only problem was he insisted on wearing an appalling long white coat all the time. He'd got it from the milkman, and he went fishing in it, cleaned the windows in it, polished the car in it. The first time Grace came she thought he was the doctor. She just couldn't understand why he was serving us dinner!'

Driving home on yet another evening, the two couples, with David at the wheel, suddenly found themselves going the wrong way down a one way street. 'Grace was sitting in the back,' said Niv, 'and as we went down the street she suddenly called out, "David – we'll get into trouble."

' "How can we get into trouble," I replied. "You own this place!" '

The late Noël Coward was another of Niv's dearest friends, and for years they had homes in Switzerland only a short distance apart. David always delighted in repeating one of his friend's 'dining' stories. Age was a topic that frequently occurred at their meetings and both men shared the same motto: 'Never resent growing older: millions are denied the privilege.'

'I try not to think of myself being any particular age,' Niv said on the eve of his sixtieth birthday. 'Otherwise you're doomed. I keep remembering what Noël Coward said to someone who was going on about the number of his friends who had died. "Personally," said Noël crisply, "I'm delighted if mine last through luncheon," '

However, David's favourite Noël Coward story – in which he himself was involved – originated from World War II. 'During the war Noël went all over the world entertaining the troops,' he said, 'and after a trip to the Middle East he wrote a book called *Middle East Diary* in which he described going into an American hospital full of what he called "snivelling little boys from Brooklyn". Well, you can imagine this did not go down well in America, and one newspaper reviewed the book under the headline, "Kick This Bum Out of The Country".

'The day after this paper appeared, Noël opened at the Marigny Theatre in Paris with Maurice Chevalier and Marlene Dietrich. Now the American troops were sure that Chevalier was a collaborator and Marlene a German spy, so adding Noël must have seemed the last straw. I was on leave from my unit in Holland at the time so I decided to go to the opening night.

'Before the perfomance began I went to see Noël in his dressing-room and told him, "You know, there are about 500 people out there and I'm afraid they are going to kill you. What are you going to do?"

'Noël was quite unperturbed. "First," he said, "I shall calm them, and then I shall sing some of my very excellent songs."

' "Well," I said, "I'll stand by the exit door because ... you know, just in case ..."

'So I went out and stood at the back by the exit. Noël came on to a deathly hush which, of course, he's not used to. A *deathly* hush. And then he looked at them and said, "Ladies and Gentlemen, and all you dear, dear snivelling little boys from Brooklyn ..." And they all just collapsed in laughter – they loved it!'

On a more poignant note, David recalled the last time he and Noël were together. 'The Christmas before he died we were all there. We were chatting about what we would do the following Christmas, and Noël spoke. "There will be no Christmas," he said. "I will not be there." He wasn't that ill, he was only seventy-two, not old.

'He orchestrated his end. There were all those revivals of his shows, and then he went to bed and died. He used to lie in bed a great deal. My wife and I went to see him. Hjordis is always upset by people who are ill. She asked him, "But Noël, what are you doing in bed?" Noel answered "I'm dying, my dear." And he did, very soon afterwards.'

On the subject of illness and his wife, David had an uncanny tale which he

Overleaf: Another role which enhanced his reputation, Phileas Fogg, in *Around the World in Eighty Days* (1956), with co-star, Cantinflas.

related to his great journalist friend Roderick Mann in 1964. 'You know Hjordis is a spook,' he said. 'A quite extraordinary girl. Did you know that she can actually smell bad health. If I'm going to be ill, she knows it. If she's going to be ill, she knows it. Way in advance. Once when we were in Rhode Island on a shoot she refused to come out with us one day, saying she knew she would be shot. We laughed and told her to be sure to wear a thick coat. "I'll come," she said, "only if you all insist." Well, we all insisted – and twenty minutes later she was shot. She got five pellets in the cheeks and seven in the neck and bosom. And there were twelve witnesses who had heard what she said earlier. How do you explain that?'

Many of Niv's friends were, of course, brought together in 1956 in Mike Todd's lavish production *Around the World in Eighty Days* which earned him excellent reviews. Two years later he confirmed his international stature in a pair of films co-starring another friend, Deborah Kerr, first in Otto Preminger's *Bonjour Tristesse* and then the outstanding *Separate Tables* which earned him his one and only Oscar.

The making of *Bonjour Tristesse* was marred – though not unduly affected – by a rare quarrel between Niv and his director, the notoriously tough Otto Preminger. Because of David's well-known equable manner, the argument between the two earned headlines in various national papers which claimed he had actually gone on strike. After filming was completed, in November 1957, Niv put the record straight in his own inimitable way.

'It happened in the Bois de Boulogne on the very first day of filming,' he recalled. 'I wasn't needed, but Otto said I was. He sent a plane to fetch me from a party I'd gone to in Deauville, 130 miles away. When I got to the Bois, Otto was blue in the face.

' "Don't walk – run," he shouted.

' "Don't shout," I said.

' "I always shout when I'm upset," he bellowed.

' "And I always sit down when I'm upset," I said. And I did.

'He was furious. Everyone expected a head-on collision on the set next day. But he beamed all over his face and said: "Have you seen our pictures in the paper? Wonderful!"

'You know, that man had gone and had a five-course dinner on his upset stomach. Me – I couldn't eat a thing. It's not the first time he'd tried to insult me. I told Jean Seberg that when he had her in tears one day. Otto overheard me. "And when my dear David," he said, "did I insult you?"

'In *The Moon is Blue*,' I told him. 'You were sitting there, your great Prussian head gleaming, your big blue eyes peering out of the dark, and you said: "Mr Niven, you are so charming off the stage. Why can't you be charming on it?"

'Otto roared. But he got his own back. He made me play one scene twenty

THIS IS THE MAJOR...WHAT DOES HE DO IN THE DARK?

THE ACTOR IS DAVID NIVEN.   THE MOTION PICTURE IS *SEPARATE/TABLES*   A HECHT-HILL-LANCASTER PRODUCTION

times! But he's a great director and marvellous once you get to know him.'

Preminger, for his part, confined his remarks about the incident to a brief, 'It was just a misunderstanding. We're the best of friends.'

Niv was always quick to pay heartfelt tribute to Deborah Kerr for her part in *Separate Tables*. He revealed just a little of the chemistry that obviously existed between them after he had received his Oscar. 'She's a dream to work with,' he said, 'because being a good actress, she's such a giggler. I can sometimes hardly look her in the eye when she giggles at me.'

Giggle the pair may have done when off-camera, but on screen they gave a most moving portrait of two sad, lonely people which proved – if anyone doubted it – that Niv was also capable of playing drama as well as comedy. Of the role, he said in 1966: 'I found it easier to do than comedy. If you're nervous while playing in drama it adds something to your performance. If you're nervous in comedy you might as well shoot yourself. You can't smile and you wind up looking like a mad rabbit.'

He also recalled feeling a bit like a 'mad rabbit' at the actual Oscar ceremony. 'I fell up the stairs as I was going to receive my award,' he said some years later. 'So when I reached the microphone I said, "I feel I must try to explain this rather big entrance. The reason I fell over was because I was so loaded ..."

'Everybody roared. They thought a self-confessed drunk was at work with the whole world watching. Of course I'd wanted to say I was loaded down with so many good luck charms that I was top heavy. But I was unable to finish that story. Absolutely disastrous!'

Another female co-star who made quite an impression on him – though in a rather different way – was Sophia Loren, with whom he co-starred with Paul Newman in *Lady L* made in 1965. Again he recounts the experience in a typically comic style. 'It would have been easy to fall in love with her while we were making the picture,' he recalled some years later. 'I mean she's an earthy bird with a beautiful bosom. Get into a scene with her and she's a joy. She gives so much. But I'll never forget that time Paul and I were supposed to met her in a brothel – one of the film sets, of course. We were having a reception there to launch the picture. Hundreds of people around, but no sign of Sophia. After half an hour, when Paul and I felt quite drained, there was a fanfare and Sophia swept in flanked by her bodyguard. She strode to a particular position in front of the canapé table, struck a pose, and immediately one spotlight hit her face from the right and another pre-set pin-spot hit her from the left.

' "Come, Daveeed. Come Paul darleeeeng," she called imperiously, holding out her arms. We had no choice but to come and stand in the semi-darkness on either side of her. A thousand cameras clicked and she was bang in the spotlight. But she really was a charming lady!' he added.

Despite the accolades that were greeting Niv's films in the early sixties, he was determined not to fall into the same trap that had spoiled his earliest successes. Indeed, an encounter he had in a London club shortly after collecting his Oscar and appearing on newspaper front pages all over the world could do nothing but help keep him on an even keel. Writing in 1957 he said, 'I was on a brief visit to London and wandered into the Naval and Military Club which I had not visited for years. I was heading for the bar when I passed an elderly, dyspeptic general who looked as if he had not moved from his chair since the days of Beau Brummell.

' "I say Niven," he muttered, barely looking up from a moth-eaten copy of *Horse and Hounds*, "I hear you're going to leave us."

' "On the contrary, sir," I said. "I'm just back. I've been in Hollywood for twenty years."

' "Really, my boy?" he said, tweaking his long, gnarled moustache, "I didn't know you had been there!"

If Niv was no longer in any danger of suffering from ego-trips, his work schedule nevertheless kept him on the move, except for his winter breaks.

In 1966 he was reunited with another old friend, John Huston, who was one of the directors on the James Bond spoof, *Casino Royale*. Their friendship has already been recorded by Niv in his books – but one story slipped the net to re-emerge while this film was being made.

'John's a great character,' he said. 'I remember when he took up hypnotism. We were at some party, and he called for a subject and of course up jumped fool Niven. There were fifty people standing about and John kept telling me: "You're getting deeper and deeper asleep, kid." Actually nothing at all was happening, but I didn't like to tell him because one likes to please. Then he suddenly stubbed out a lighted cigarette in the palm of my hand and I let out a wild shriek of pain!'

It was not just for his friends that Niv could put on such improbable performances. In the summer of 1968, his now grown-up younger son, Jamie, married a former deb, Fernanda Wetherill, on Long Island, New York. A high point of the festivities was a party that the Nivens gave for the other guests, some of whom they knew and many more they did not. 'I stationed myself at the door,' David recalled afterwards, 'and as each person came in I said, "I'm going to tell you four things. 1. I am the host. 2. My wife is at the bar waiting to greet you. 3. You'll find where to sit from that little paper behind you. 4. There are 120 of us and only one loo." It was a very good way of separating the gigglers from the rest!'

For a man who was always so ready to laugh at himself, it came as something of a surprise in March 1971 when he refused to appear on Eamonn Andrews' famous programme, *This Is Your Life*. Certainly it was unfortunate that someone either inadvertently or deliberately told Niv what

81

One of the many
hilarious moments
from *Lady L*
(1965) with the
beautiful Sophia
Loren.

was being planned and he reacted sharply, 'Not on *your* life!'

Of course, whatever revelations the programme might have produced, they could hardly have matched the incredible impact of Niv's book, *The Moon's a Balloon* when it was published later that same year. The success of this work – and its successor – remain without parallel in the history of show business autobiographies, and their combined sales are now over ten million copies and still continuing.

He had, as I have described, already written that earlier novel as well as the various newspaper articles, but he was totally unprepared for the staggering success which greeted his work. He showed a nervousness and excitement about how the public would react to his work that was in striking contrast to his usual cool and sophisticated manner. He was almost breathless waiting for information on sales and reviews.

Later, David was to confess that writing the books was agony, and he was worried all along that these works which were, at their most basic level, essentially a succession of funny stories drawn from his career, would prove too preposterous – even ridiculous – to the average reader. He need not have worried: he had found a formula that has become the envy of all professional writers, not to mention other film stars who have entered the literary stakes. And, though he had named names, he had not stooped into the mire of scandal and gossip which usually permeates show business books.

The credit for persuading Niv to write *The Moon's a Balloon* rests with his close friends from the literary world: journalist Roderick Mann, author Irwin Shaw, and the barrister-playwright, John Mortimer. All knew his spellbinding skill as a raconteur and Roderick Mann, in particular, had more than once urged him to write his memoirs. 'I keep telling David Niven that he should write his autobiography,' Mann wrote in his column of 4 September 1966. 'He keeps telling me that he will; he will. But he doesn't.'

After the successful launching of the book, Niv was ready to talk about just how hard it had been to put pen to paper. 'It began as a bit of a joke. I thought it would make a few chums laugh. I got terribly depressed doing it: often thought, "Why am I bothering with this nonsense?"

'A journalist pal of mine had said one day he couldn't interview me any more because he knew too much about me already. He suggested *I* should write it all down, so I did.

'Once it was underway it began to unfold itself, but I still had to conquer the fact that I'll do anything to avoid writing. First of all, I only do it when the weather is bad, so that writing doesn't interfere with anything, and living mostly in the South of France, I don't get too much bad weather. If a 747 flies over, that's worth at least another ten minutes to me because I go out into the garden and look up at the sky trails. Then I'll take a look round the garden, check the boiler – anything not to go back and get on.

One of Niv's
greatest passions
when not working
was to head for
the ski slopes of
Switzerland.

'I write anywhere. Did a lot of *The Moon's a Balloon* in Malaysia. But I can't type. I tried to dictate into a machine, but that was misery because of the boredom of my voice when I played it back. Then I rented a lady from Nice who was so horrified by the four letter words that she gave in her notice. A very attractive American girl, who roared with laughter at everything I said, was worse, because I found myself writing in order to make the secretary laugh. She had to go. I've wound up with the children's notebooks and pencils and did it all in longhand. In the end, though, I enjoyed it. The most fascinating part was lifting up the stones in my memory and finding what came wriggling out ...'

Apart from 'lifting up stones in his memory', Niv was also able to help himself remember people and events through the scrapbooks of cuttings he had kept during his career. And having had the chance of reading a great many of these clippings which range across half a century, I found it particularly interesting the way many anecdotes had been transposed from the newspaper page to the book with hardly a word changed. This, of course, made it easier for me to spot the stories he had told but not put to autobiographical service for use in this book.

When sales of 'my dear old moon' – as he later came to call the work – made it obvious Niv had created a genuine bestseller, his relief was immediately evident. 'I can't tell you what gratification I got when the book was successful,' he said in November 1978. 'I couldn't bear the thought of all that work for something nobody bought. Of course, my film career gives me a huge, unfair advantage. I can go on all those talk shows and flog my books while real writers starve.'

Such a modest view of his talent was typical of David, who told another interviewer that same month: 'If you're lucky enough to be able to polish minimal talent into a career, then you should be on your knees every morning thanking God for it. We've all of us had our modicum of pleasure and tragedy. Funny things happen to everybody. But some people have been kissed by the Almighty and want to record the event. And I swear to you that everything in that book happened to me. It would be unforgivable – and very foolish – to steal anything. Someone would catch you out.'

In the years which followed, Niv remained delighted with the success of his book and, of course, he proved it had been no mere flash in the pan with the sequel, *Bring On the Empty Horses* which appeared in 1975. He was deluged with fan mail all the time, but was not too taken aback when some people complained that *The Moon's a Balloon* was rather shocking.

'Among the batch of letters I found this package,' he recalled. 'Inside I found just the cover of the hardback of *The Moon's a Balloon*. The pages had been ripped out, and there was a note telling me that the filth between the covers had been removed! Filth ... my life story!

Amid all the drama, the irrepressible Niv still burst through – as in *The Elusive Pimpernel* (1949).

'I wrote to the woman – she'd had the nerve to put her name and address – and said I was terribly sorry she was upset by the bad language, but pointed out that there was no way, if I was to write truly about soldiers and prostitutes and actors, to do so without using four-letter words. I probably won't hear from her again, but I hope my reply calmed her a little.'

Many other readers wanted to know who was 'Kira Triandpyllapopulous' to whom the book was dedicated. Another Nessie, some wondered? When David revealed the truth there were some very embarrassed folk around. 'A lot of people said very straight-faced, "Oh, yes, I knew her. She's a Greek actress isn't she?" But the truth is Kira is my dog, an Afghan hound, and the rest of the name I made up. The dedication is just a piece of fun!'

As was his nature, David quickly redressed the balance at his own expense with a new story not included in either book. It happened, he said, at the time John Wayne's wife was giving birth to one of their sons. 'I didn't realise it,' said Niv, 'but apparently she had the most appalling labour. I sent a cable that read simply: "Congratulations. I thought it was wind." Then I heard the Duke was looking for me, I had to steer clear of him for months!'

David's literary triumph made him still more in demand on television chat shows as well as a lecturer, talking – inevitably perhaps – about the great days of Hollywood. In July 1973 he was delightfully reminiscing about this aspect of his life: with humour, of course. 'I'm actually one of the few people still breathing who was in Hollywood then,' he said. 'People seem to be riveted by stories of Gable and Bogart and Garbo. I can give up to twenty-seven lectures in thirty-one days. Absolutely hysterical. Going from Minneapolis, Jacksonville, Florida. All over the place.

'I drive up to the town. I'm met by the sponsor. His wife's just been to the hairdresser to get her blue rinse. His daughter wants to be in the movies. They greet me and take me to my room. It's the Holiday Inn. The Bamboo Suite. The same in every town.

'I won't lecture anywhere near Los Angeles. It's too close to home. Actually these people may be a bit square, but you can't put them down because they're so sweet. I tell them dull stories about Europe. Then I tell them dull stories about Hollywood. Then I finish up and go on to the next town.'

Niv was also asked to be one of the masters of ceremonies at that same year's Oscar awards. Though he was not up for a prize he nonetheless managed to be the centre of the evening's funniest moment – when a streaker ran across the stage.

'There were the usual back-stage mix-ups,' he recalls. 'Liza and Barbra having to share the same dressing-room, John Huston turning up tired and emotional, the usual things. Toward the end, after all the awards had been weepingly accepted, I had to introduce Liz Taylor.

'Suddenly I heard a shriek of laughter. I thought, oh shit, she's come on topless. I turned around and just caught a glimpse of this naked ass running off the stage! No one believed I hadn't arranged it.'

Another surprise from David after the ceremonies was the revelation of a secret ambition he still nursed. 'I've one more ambition before I die,' he said. 'I've won an Oscar and written a bestseller. Now I want to have a painting in the Louvre. I don't somehow think I'll make it. The nearest I'll get to it, I suppose, is to hang one in the "loo".'

It came as a surprise to most people that David enjoyed painting and had, in fact, done so for years. Certainly, it was known that he had an enviable collection of paintings, but an actual dauber *himself*? Niv went straight into his grab-bag of stories. 'You know William Buckley, the American political commentator?' he asked. 'Great chum! He's the worst amateur painter in the world. I can say that, because I'm the second worst. He was staying with us when Marc Chagall visited us. In his eighties, wonderful man! I begged Bill not to show him any of his paintings. He knocks off nine a night, and they all look like the bottom of Lake Eyre.

'But the moment they were introduced, Bill buttonholed Chagall and brought out his latest ghastly effort. Chagall studied it for a minute or two, then he shook his head and said "poor paint"!'

Niv also expressed a desire to write a screenplay and maintained that John Mortimer had constantly urged him to get on with it. 'In actual fact,' he confided in 1975, 'I've been working on one for years. I've got this group of people trapped in a lighthouse. But more characters keep arriving and its getting very crowded.'*

However, according to George Greenfield, his literary agent, the play was a 'joke fantasy'. 'He had a habit of teasing journalists by telling them improbable stories,' George told me in September 1983.

Another delightful story he served up in August 1976 concerned a film

---

*Another nautical story – but true – concerns two of Niv's other Hollywood 'chums', Robert Wagner and his wife, Natalie Wood, who was later to die so tragically in a boating accident. There was no suggestion however of such a grim episode when David related the following story in February 1977 about how *he* nearly drowned when sailing with the Wagners. 'We'd been out for a day's fishing,' he said, 'and Wagner was manoeuvring his great monster alongside this small berth. He was wearing his cap with "Captain" written on it, and I was the only crew. Wagner called to me not to jump too soon. Well, of course, I did, and fell into the water. Wagner didn't even notice that his only crewman wasn't with him any longer. There he was, calling out instructions, while I was floundering around trying like hell to get out! Then he spotted me and thought I had broken my leg. To his utmost credit, he was about to jump overboard and leave his boat – his life's savings – but I made it in the end and, once I'd dried out, we had a good laugh over the incident!'

Three faces of
Niv — here proving
that he can play
any kind of role
from a chauffeur
to a gardener,
and even a crusty
old aristocrat.
And all for one
film, *Candleshoe*
made in 1977!

script he said he had commissioned called *The Last White Man*. 'I got those two marvellous writers from *Private Eye*, John Wells and Barry Fantoni to write it with me in mind for the leading role. It opens in Christie's with the Crown Jewels being auctioned. They are identified in the catalogue as "The Property of a Lady".

'Outside there stands an old fellow in a tattered Gannex mac, holding up a sign: "Wife and secretary to support",' Niv adds. Then raising a mischievous eyebrow he asked, 'Do you think we dare make it?'

Niv's fascination with the written word came to a temporary halt in 1977, however, when the eldest of his two adopted daughters, Kristina, then eighteen, was involved in a near-fatal car crash in Switzerland and lay in a coma for some time. It was a traumatic experience that took its toll of him and Hjordis. They spoke of it to no-one but their closest friends, but finally David emerged relieved and happier in the summer of 1979. Mixed with his relief was the inevitable quip as if to assure everyone he was back to normal.

'When the accident happened I just couldn't write a line,' he said. 'She had a total wipe-out of memory and it needed a miracle for her to recover. How could I sit down and write funny jokes with that on my mind?

'Happily, she is right as rain now, although she only had her last operation recently; they put a steel pin in her leg.

'We had her eighteenth birthday party in the South of France the other day and Prince Rainier and Princess Grace came over for it with their son Albert. I just wish I'd had a camera handy, because during dinner Kristina dropped a pair of diamond earrings on the terrace and there were Grace and Rainier and the rest of us crawling round on our hands and knees looking for them! It was quite a sight!

'Now that Kristina is all right, I've been able to start writing again. Although it's still hard and I don't mind admitting I'm absolutely terrified of having a flop. After the success of the last two, what if this one's no good? What I'll do is leave the final decision to my publishers. If they decide it's a load of old rubbish, then I'll forget it.'

But there was little chance that Niv's new work would prove a 'load of old rubbish', although he admitted that he had abandoned his autobiographical style to try a novel once again. Inevitably, of course, there would be more than a little of himself in it, but he hoped to carry off the plot and dialogue with more skill than he felt he had shown in his earlier work. His provisional title was *Make It Smaller and Move It To the Left*.

'I'm basing it partly on my painting days,' he confided in 1979 while filming in England. 'When I was on Goldwyn's blacklist in Hollywood I decided to be a painter. I enrolled at an art school and the first model I used was an ex-ballerina who had boobs like a spaniel's ears. I finished very quickly and the lady running the art class said afterwards I was meant to spend five weeks on the painting.

' "But I've given it all I can," I replied. However, another art teacher told me, "Make it smaller and move it to the left." Hence the title.'

With his weakness for being distracted, there were times when the writing did not go well. He recalled one day when he was working on the story at Cap Ferrat. 'I was totally stuck,' he said, 'so I wandered up to the old Somerset Maugham villa for inspiration. He used to write in a small summer house in the grounds. I thought I'd whiff the wonderful aroma in the summer house and that might give me inspiration. A couple of houses are now being built on the estate but the little summer house is still there. I walked in and found it was being used as a lavatory by the Algerian building workers. No inspiration!'

But Niv's love story, set partly in London during the Blitz and partly in Hollywood, did get finished and was finally published in the autumn of 1981. The title, though, had been changed to *Go Slowly, Come Back Quickly*. Although not a success in the same astonishing mould of the two autobiographies, it sold extremely well and was well received by the critics. Reviewers liked Niv's references to Hollywood as 'a glut of inferiority complexes' where 'people talk their way up the ladder and find they have vertigo when they get there.' *The Times* felt the book 'distils humanity and elegance, stirring and shaking'.

David made publication time another joyous event with a fund of new stories. One tale concerned his butler who had been offered a huge increase to go and work for someone else. But such was Niv's determination to keep the man that the fellow had to resort to desperate means to get himself fired. So he bored a hole in one of Hjordis' cups in order to drench her when she drank her morning tea!

Another recalled the day when David had gone to watch a balloon race in the mountains near his Swiss home. Suddenly he had found himself dragged into one of the baskets because everyone was convinced after seeing him in *Around the World in Eighty Days* that he must be an expert. 'But in fact,' he said, 'it was written into my contract that I never had to be more than four feet six inches off the ground. And I wasn't!'

He'd also collected an amusing yarn about his long-standing friend Laurence Olivier. 'Like everyone else I was very moved by Larry's emotional and fine-sounding speech at the Oscar Ceremony in 1979. But when I saw him afterwards he confessed that although he'd practised the speech beforehand, he blew it halfway through.

'Since Larry had faced the same problem before on stage with Shakespeare he knew just what to do. "Hardly anyone knows the lines well enough to challenge you," he told me, "so if you forget you just bluff your way through." And that's what he did with my Oscar speech. Which is why it

sounded wonderful and moved people like Jon Voight to tears – though it actually made no sense at all!'

Another old friend who became the victim of a Niven practical joke was Douglas Fairbanks Jnr. Niv recalled the event vividly. 'I was in London with the day off,' he said, 'so I called my old chum Fairbanks whom I hadn't seen for two years. I said I was from the *Daily Mail*, James Jossop, working for Nigel Dempster, the gossip columnist. I told Fairbanks that we'd just been in touch with Mr David Niven, and that when we'd told him about his – Fairbanks' – great success on stage, he'd answered, "Well, I think he's a bloody awful actor." I invited him to say what he thought of David Niven.

'Fairbanks said, "Well, he's probably right. I probably am. He is a great friend of mine, and occasionally he does say some things rather too hastily. But he is a splendid man, and a magnificent actor ..."

'And I thought, Oh, God, how dreadful: all these paeons of praise coming out of this insulted man. So I won't be doing anything like that again.

'But Fairbanks? Oh, he almost died laughing when I owned up. He was so happy about it, when we had lunch, that he called some friends in New York right away to tell them!'

It was, of course, rare for David to tell a story against anyone other than himself: almost as rare as it was for him to talk about the charities and causes to which he unobtrusively gave his time, energy and money over the years. He was, in fact, an active worker for the Salk Cancer Foundation in America and got great fun from promoting the Jersey Wildlife Organisation. One of his very best uncollected stories has to do with this worthy body.

'I was performing this opening ceremony for them,' he said in 1979. 'The theme was that gentlemen gorillas should be allowed to mate with lady gorillas while they are in captivity.

'Well, I made this frightfully solemn speech and everyone was rocking with laughter. I couldn't think why until I happened to turn round. And there were the lady and gentlemen in question mating away like mad in the background!'

Behind the amiable façade, Niv was, of course, a devoted family man, equally proud of his two older boys and the adopted girls. Jamie, the younger son, has become a New York investment banker, while David Jnr followed Niv's footsteps into the world of films, though as a producer rather than an actor. He now holds one of the top executive jobs at MGM.

Niv and David Jnr actually had the pleasure of working together on two films: *Escape to Athena* in 1979 and *Better Late Than Never* in 1981 which was to prove, tragically, Niv's last starring role. *Escape to Athena* not only brought father and son together on a movie set but also took them back to an island they had visited years before.

'When the boys were quite young we toured the Greek Islands,' David

Like father like son – David Niven Jnr follows his father into the film business, though as a producer rather than a star. They are photographed here with Hjordis at a gala evening in Monaco.

95

reminisced during the shooting of the picture in which he very appropriately played an archaeologist. 'Apart from the beauty of the islands we got a taste for archaeology. I still have at home a collection of the things we dug up. I suppose that's where "Junior" gained his initial fondness for coming here. Then I did one of my favourite pictures, *The Guns of Navarone** right here in Rhodes.

'So you see he didn't have to sell me on the idea. I accepted immediately, although as an afterthought I did say, "Send me a script ..." And what better luck could I ask for than working for my son? You know the money's coming in the right direction!'

Niv also explained why he referred to his son as 'Junior'. 'When he was small, it was "little David and big David". Then when he got as big as I, it became "Young David and Old David". Now you know, I couldn't stand that!'

On hearing this, David Niven Jnr confined himself to a grin the splitting image of his father's and a single remark, 'Really, it's nepotism in reverse.' The same good humour between them was also evident when they were reunited in the South of France in October 1981 to make *Better Late Than Never*, with another of Niv's old friends, Bryan Forbes, as director. Once again the attraction of working in such a delightful spot as the Riviera – which he knew well – had made it an easy choice for David: a factor emphasised by his son.

'There's not a lot of point coming here,' explained David Jnr, 'if you're going to shut yourself away in a studio. And we've been lucky with the weather. If we have had any problems at all I suppose it was when we filmed on a topless beach at Juan les Pins. That sent some of the crew into a bit of a

---

*It was while making this picture in April 1960 that David Niven revealed that he had turned down the chance to star in one of the most famous – if notorious – films of the era, *Lolita*. 'I was offered *Lolita*,' he told Roderick Mann, 'and thought for weeks before deciding I couldn't do it. It would have been a tremendous challenge, but I honestly lacked the courage to do it. The truth is, I suppose, that I am associated with certain sorts of parts, and audiences might have been shocked to see me in a film like *Lolita*. Audiences react curiously, you know. After I made *Happy Anniversary* in which a man admitted that he had had an affair with his wife before he married her, I got shoals of angry letters from fans saying, "How could you!" ' The part of Humbert Humbert was, of course, taken by James Mason who played it with great success. Three other famous films in which Niven might have appeared were Charles Laughton's *The Private Life of Henry VIII* (he failed the test), *The African Queen* (dropped by Warner Bros in 1938 where he was signed to play the part later immortalised by Humphrey Bogart) and *Baden-Powell*, the story of the founder of the Boy Scout Movement in which he was to be B.P., until the unexpected death of producer Cecil B. de Mille in 1959.

tailspin. They couldn't stop staring. But after a few days you get used to it.'

There were as ever amusing anecdotes to be gleaned from the indefatigable Niv. 'Graham Greene, who lives nearby, came over to see us on the set one day,' he explained. 'But I'm such an admirer of his that I couldn't bring myself to mention the fact that I'd also written a few books.' (As if he needed to!)

A magnificent villa at Antibes which belonged to a wealthy Englishman and was used for some scenes also provided him with another story. 'The owner was rather baffled by us,' he said. 'Looking at the unit he asked Bryan Forbes, "Why do you need so many people to do something so trivial?" And he also asked, "When you're doing it where do you put all your models?" He meant us, the actors!'

Bryan Forbes retains the warmest memories of *Better Late Than Never*. 'Niv was as easy-going as ever, but had the discipline of somebody brought up in the old tough school of pre-war Hollywood. He was a compulsive worker, always prepared to believe that his long run of luck was about to end. I have a suspicion that this recurrent fear, so characteristic of many actors, hastened his end.'

After completing the picture, Niv set off on a promotion tour of America for his novel, and there can be little doubt that his health began to deteriorate under the strain. He had never been easy on himself, and because of this it was to be some time before anyone outside his family circle realised he had contracted a fatal disease.

David Niven's last months were the subject of relentless, though in many instances, well-meaning speculation about his obviously failing condition. There were headlines that he had suffered a stroke – the source of this information apparently being his friend Cary Grant. In September 1982 he responded over the phone from Cap Ferrat with something matching his old humour: 'I am happy to tell you that although I am cold having been called in from swimming outside, I will take a £10,000 bet with Cary or anyone else who says I've had a stroke. It's a total fallacy.'

And, of course, it was. But stories that he was having trouble speaking were nearer the truth, and were confirmed during the shooting of scenes for his brief appearances in *The Curse of the Pink Panther*.

David Niven Jnr endeavoured to assure his father's friend that he was taking good care of himself and was even occupying himself with another book. A fact confirmed by his agent George Greenfield who told me that by early 1983 Niv had written 30,000 words of a novel set in modern times involving guerrillas and terrorist action. Although destined never to be finished, it showed that none of Niv's legendary determination to keep working had deserted him.

Nor had his courage or his humour. For in February 1983 he came to

Tragic illness kills film star

NIVEN'S BRAVE LAST FIGHT

By DAVID LEWIN and PETER SHERIDAN

DAVID NIVEN died yesterday after displaying debonair courage to the end.

The veteran film star—and best-selling author—knew two months ago that death was approaching.

Up to that time, despite the wasting illness which reduced his body to skeletal proportions, he could still swim in the pool at his home at Cap Ferrat, the South of France.

But in the last few weeks the most he could manage was to go with a ring in the shallow end. 'Even then he would smile and wave and blow kisses,' Doreen Hawkins, an old friend and frequent visitor, remembered.

Energetic

What was so awful for him as his body wasted was his declining ability to speak — for Niven was a born raconteur.

His friends would sit with him while he moved his lips and tried to formulate the words which constantly eluded him. Just about the last thing he said before he died — and it took great powers of concentration for those with him to hear him — were the words 'It's so boring.'

And boring it was for the man who had been so energetic. He tried to alleviate the boredom by writing — laboriously in longhand — another book. But the words came slowly, not because he didn't know what he wanted to say but because his hand no longer had the power to hold the pen.

Niven, who was 73, left the South of France three weeks ago for his mountain chalet in Switzerland,

Turn to Page 2, Col 6

Royal smiles in the sunshine

Happy couple . . . the Prince and Princess after the ceremony yesterday

By STEPHEN LYNAS and JOHN HAMSHIRE

Princess Michael's dream comes true

PRINCESS Michael of Kent was welcomed back into the Roman Catholic Church at the quietest of royal ceremonies yesterday — exactly two years after the pomp and splendour when Prince Charles married Lady Diana Spencer.

The 15-minute blessing of their marriage took place in the tiny, wood-lined private chapel in Archbishop House at Westminster Cathedral where Cardinal Basil Hume normally says his private Mass.

As the 38-year-old Princess walked hand in hand out into the sunshine with her husband Prince Michael of Kent, her quiet smile showed her joy that her five-year fight to be accepted back in the Church was over The Princess, wearing a

Turn to Page 2, Col. 1

RITA HAYWORTH

Secrets of a Love Goddess

RITA HAYWORTH was the star who had everything . . . the supreme sex symbol they called the Love Goddess, and whose glittering career was littered with scandal and sensation in her life off screen.

But today she lives alone in a New York apartment and few except her daughter, Princess Yasmin, are in touch with her.

Now Princess Yasmin talks for the first time of what the years have done to one of Hollywood's most beautiful stars.

Read the extraordinary story. Next week. And, of course, ONLY in the Mail.

London to the Wellington Hospital for tests and an examination. And to amuse the reporters he must have known were hovering outside trying to find out what was going on, he registered himself as 'David Snooks'.

But there was no laughing his way out of the insidious illness that now had hold of him, and with quiet resignation he returned home to Switzerland where he must have known the end could not be far off. The Motor Neurone Disease which slowly turned his body into a skeleton also deprived him of the even more precious gift of his voice. Telling stories, collecting gossip, became increasingly difficult. 'Perhaps it is because I have talked too much all my life!' he managed to joke with John Mortimer on what was to be their last reunion. Then speech became impossible. 'It's so boring,' were his last recorded words.

He still managed to send the occasional letter, however, and another friend, Anthony Quayle received 'a funny little note' dictated by Niv from his bed a few weeks before the end. 'It said, "Whatever you do, don't get this disease – I can't talk, I can't write, I can't do anything." He also said he had discovered what he'd always suspected, that he was a coward – but that was not true. He had great courage.'*

And then on 29 July 1983 David Niven slipped quietly away, his redoubtable will still enabling him to give a typical thumbs-up sign to his very last visitor, his nephew, Michael Wranadah. Niv was seventy-three. The star whose career had stretched almost unbelievably from The Golden Age of Hollywood to the Video Era, was dead.

He had made his exit rather in the manner of the best piece of advice he said he had ever been given: 'Turn up on time, get the jokes right, take the cheque and go home.'

But though Niv might have left the party he always believed life to be – the memory lingers on. Not only in the thoughts of his friends whose tributes are to be found in these pages, but also in the minds of the uncounted millions to whom he gave enormous pleasure on the screen and on the printed page, who will probably always remember him as 'The Last Gentleman Actor' ...

Few film stars make front-page, headline news when they die – but Niv did. A sure sign of his fame and immense popularity.

*In September 1983 Anthony Quayle and a number of David Niven's other friends in conjunction with Hjordis Niven set up an appeal on behalf of the Motor Neurone Disease Association. The group – including Bryan Forbes, Sir Laurence Olivier, Sir John Mills, Deborah Kerr, John Mortimer and Douglas Fairbanks Jnr – felt that the disease, which has no cure, should be better known. They wrote, "David Niven was never slow to come forward and give of his talents for the aid of others less fortunate, and we felt that, numbered amongst his countless admirers, there might be some who would wish to repay him in this manner."

'Dear Trubshawe'

by David Niven

The following two 'letters' appeared in the London Daily Express of 17 September 1946 and 2 November 1946, introduced thus:

David Niven, film star and wartime lieutenant-colonel, is an incurable letter writer to friends at home. Here, in England, they dine out on his news, comments, life and sparkle. Now David Niven writes for readers everywhere in dispatches direct from Hollywood.

The letters are addressed to 'Dear Trubshawe', David Niven's best friend, Arthur Michael Trubshawe, the publican of the Lamb Inn, Hoe, near Battle Sussex. He is an ex-regular officer, Tory 'blue as blue could be', bad cricketer, bad shot – but loves hunting – an institution to his friends, and a good luck name to Niven – he hopes. Trubshawe is 6ft 3ins, wears Edwardian-cut clothes – 'my favourite period' – pearl tie-pin, red carnation, and a moustache 7½ ins long. They first met in 1930 – in the cricket pavillion in Malta. 'We found we laughed at the same things and got into trouble at the same time,' he says.

Lifelong friends, Niv and Michael Trubshawe, photographed during one of David's visits to England.

Hollywood, Monday

Dear Trubshawe,

WHEN YOU ASK me to write, giving you all the news, views and wisdom of Hollywood, I don't think you realise exactly what you are doing to me. To start with, every studio, a large percentage of the directors and most of the stars employ highly-paid lawyers who lurk behind them twenty-four hours a day thumbing expectantly through the libel laws of the United States and just waiting for somebody like me to open his mouth too wide.

Much as I would enjoy dipping my fingers into the paper bag of my local knowledge and distributing the crumbs of my information to the pigeons who are your inquisitive friends, I shall have to be very, very careful how I set about this. I have no wish to end my screen career making background shots for other people's prison pictures.

I have always made it a golden rule never to knock other actors, for the obvious reason that I am not nearly a good enough one myself to withstand the recoil. Conversely, I am ashamed to admit that words of praise, where other actors are concerned, usually flow from me like glue. I am, therefore, somewhat surprised to find myself gibbering and twittering with excitement over the performances of Ingrid Bergman and Cary Grant in *Notorious*.

This Hitchcock picture is really good, and the love scenes are the best, the most beautifully played, and the best directed that I have seen on the screen. Of the other artists about whom you seemed in your letter to be particularly anxious to hear news, Rex Harrison has scored a great personal success in *Anna and the King of Siam*. Beautiful Vivien Leigh is, of course, one of the top box office attractions over here, so *Caesar and Cleopatra* is doing tremendous business. *Henry V* is a smash hit; so, between them, Mr and Mrs Olivier must be putting up a world's record for family popularity.

The recipe for this is as follows: Take Mr Olivier's fantastic success with the Old Vic Company in New York, mix with that the beauty and bravery of his 'Henry', showing all over the United States, now add Mrs Olivier's triumph every time she appears on the American screen, stir slowly and season with their own personal charm and power to make everybody who comes into contact with them love them. Pour liberally, never allowing to cool, and you have the perfect mixture for promoting admiration in American hearts for British art and artists.

Ann Todd arrived last week and I happened to be in New York at the time. We had supper together the first night she was there, and she was as full of enthusiasm as a child. She had spent the day window shopping, stepping inside, being appalled at the prices, and stepping outside again. Then in the evening she and Nigel Tangye, her husband, went to see the great Broadway musical hit *Carousel*. After that Nigel delivered her to a grateful Niven and went off to attend some business meeting on her behalf.

She ordered a fruit salad and got it – American style. That means the same as an ordinary salad, complete with lettuce and tomatoes and so forth, but sitting up on top is some fruit. It shook her considerably, but she was undaunted and soon climbed outside it.

She is going to make a picture for Hitchcock with Gregory Peck – as nice a set-up as an actress could want, and one which she richly deserves after *Seventh Veil*.

Robert Donat is a great favourite over here, but all complain that they don't see enough of his pictures. The same complaint could safely be made in England.

Margaret Lockwood arrived and at the request of local cameraman struck the traditional pose of all visiting actresses – that of balancing precariously on the ship's rail displaying shapely legs and waving to some object far above the ship. I often wonder what it is they wave at; I suppose it's somebody in a skyscraper near by or perhaps a passing seagull.

She is going to make a picture at Universal. That's a very pleasant place to work, and incidentally the whole studio fell in love with Patricia Roc when she was making a picture there a short time ago.

Danny Kaye is probably the most sensational comedian to appear over here for the last ten years. Before the war he was entertaining at the Dorchester in London where he tells me ruefully that he didn't think he went down very well. Perhaps he wasn't so good then – he's terrific now.

You will be glad to know that British pictures are enjoying a tremendous upswing in popularity over here. Wherever I go – and I don't mean only in Hollywood, but all over this enormous country – I always hear the same thing. 'How wonderful British pictures are these days!'

Nobody in the world is more violently anxious than I am that British pictures should soar up to the heights of world popularity and stay there but on the other hand the fact remains that, with regard to personnel at any rate, the British film industry was pampered during the war years whereas the Hollywood industry was hampered. This probably sounds peculiar to you and I can almost hear you ordering another furious half pint to steady yourself, but it happens to be true. You see there were no 'reserved occupations' in the American film industry. Actors, producers, directors, cameramen and technicians were just called up for service and that was that. In England, however, producers, directors, cameramen and key technicians were all 'reserved' and so of course were actors – provided they remain actively employed at their job of acting.

Some of the finest Hollywood directors were away for years in the Army and the local scene will soon be brightened considerably when the productions of Frank Capra, William Wyler, John Ford, George Stevens, John Huston and Garson Kanin appear once more on the screen.

Among the actors, old favourites (but by no means old men) have now been demobilised and have finished top-class productions so you will soon again be seeing Jimmy Stewart, Robert Taylor, Tyrone Power, Henry Fonda, Melvyn Douglas and many others. All of this adds up to a healthy competition and without that we would all be sunk. Just imagine if Mr Austin and Mr Morris and Mr Rolls and Mr Royce had not looked out the window one day and said 'We can all do as well as Mr Ford!'

Goodbye for now I will write again soon.

David

Hollywood, Friday

Dear Trubshawe,

Thank you for your letter. The incredibly heavy hint contained therein did not pass unnoticed, and I have now obtained the necessary half-dozen pairs of nylons for you. The fact that you wanted them for all different sizes seemed a little peculiar at first, but I suppose every wise fisherman keeps a good assortment of bait on hand.

Hollywood, too, is still playing games after dinner, and the one that I enjoy most is known as the 'drawing game'. I played it last night at the house of my next-door neighbour, Douglas Fairbanks. Two teams were selected, and a blackboard was set up. Each team then concocted a question for each member of the opposition. These were written down, each on a separate slip of paper.

Next an official timekeeper was nominated. This happened to be a visitor from New York on his first trip to Hollywood, who remained completely stunned throughout the entire performance.

The first member of our opposing team went into bat – Jimmy Stewart. He was handed a piece of chalk, a duster, and the piece of paper containing the question which he was required to draw on the blackboard. The rest of his team sat round hoping to guess what he would try to depict, and our team, of course, settled down to do a little quiet heckling.

Jimmy's question was one word: 'reconnaissance'. He shied like a frightened mustang, but put up a very fair show. First he made one distinct mark, which his team guessed meant that the question contained only one word. After this, much work alternated between the chalk and the duster as the poor man tried to draw anything that might give his over-anxious and noisy team the necessary clue.

He drew what our team thought was a passable armoured car, but which his team guessed as either a battleship or Mr Churchill smoking a cigar. Then he tried to draw the plan of a military formation on the ground complete with some little blobs far out in front. This did not penetrate their numbskulls, and his effort was greeted with cries of 'Children's toys?' 'Crossword puzzles?' 'Squatters?'

He gave up the Army and tried his own element – the Air Force. Then, believe it or not, we were treated to the incredible spectacle of this great bomber hero losing his head and being unable to draw anything remotely resembling an airplane.

Finally, he drew an egg-shaped balloon, beneath which dangled a bucket attached apparently by a very old pair of sock suspenders and containing two men in top hats.

This shook the team considerably, and for a moment they showed signs of turning into a surly and mutinous mob. Suddenly, with a flash of genius, Jimmy drew spectacles on one of the men in the bucket and, with a smug gesture, put a huge question mark in the middle of the balloon itself.

That was enough. 'Jules Verne?' 'Stratosphere?' yelled his team. 'Looking at the world through rose-coloured spectacles?' Impatiently Jimmy pointed to the mark denoting one word only. 'They are looking for something,' shrieked Annabella. 'Explorers?' screamed Anita Colby. But Ronald Colman got it in the end – 'Reconnaissance'.

'Right,' roared our team. 'How long, timekeeper?'

'Four and a half minutes,' said the man from New York in the same tone of voice as that employed by a disgruntled helper in a kindergarten.

Now it became our turn to bat. To open the innings we selected no less a man than Clark Gable. You would think that here would be a foundation of great strength on which to build the monument of our success. It was not to be. This first actor, this intrepid war airman, this magnificent specimen of manhood, the moment the chalk was placed in his hand disintegrated before our eyes, and when he caught a glimpse of the paper he became a gibbering idiot.

An easy 'question' too, as we subsequently discovered. Two words: 'Antiphlogistine poultice'.

What did the man do to help us guess that? Nothing! For at least a minute he just stood there and shook like a blancmange. Then suddenly he was galvanised into action. He attacked the blackboard like a maniac. He broke two fingernails and three pieces of chalk before anything of note materialised. At last he produced a pear-shaped man lying on his back with what looked like a pile of books in the middle of his stomach. Smoke was seen to be pouring out of the top of this pile. Rex Harrison suggested that it was a sausage with a piece of cheese on it. Douglas Fairbanks was sure it was meant to be the headmaster of Eton College depressed by his own knowledge, and I said it looked like a cross between a street accident and two pounds of cold halibut.

This last drew a terrifying scowl from the artist. But he did further bestir himself, and used the duster to great effect. Again he attacked the

blackboard. Fingernails and pieces of chalk covered the furniture with a fine dust. The duster was flapping like the towel in any corner of any boxing ring between any two rounds. The blackboard remained a virginal black.

Suddenly a look of horrible cunning distorted the famous features. He crouched behind a sofa like a fuzzy-wuzzy before the walls of Khartoum, and, holding the chalk like a poisoned dart, he slowly stalked the blackboard. Discarding his former robust tactics, he drew two thin, spidery lines. 'Two words', we roared. He nodded happily. He then drew a square with a cross in the middle of it and looked expectant. We looked blank. He drew a stick down one side of the square.

'It's a flag', from Jennifer Jones. 'Red Cross', yelled Donald Budge. Gable nodded so violently he cricked his neck. Now we were getting warm. It was something of two words to do with the Red Cross. Suggestions like 'food parcel' and 'hospital nurse' were treated with scorn by our man, but when William Powell muttered 'medical supplies', he was transformed. Chalk and duster worked overtime. Dust flew.

When the air cleared a little a gasp of surprise and disappointment went up from our team. For there, slightly older and a good deal fatter than before, was the same pear-shaped individual with the smoking pile of books on his stomach.

David O. Selznick proceeded to enumerate the clues so far. 'It's something to do with medical supplies and it's hot and it's in the middle of a man's stomach,' he stated.

Gable flew to the blackboard and drew a great looping arrow from the top of the smoking books and hurled it underneath the man's chin.

'On his chest,' corrected our team's logical mind.

From then on it was easy. 'Mustard plaster,' yelled Rex Harrison. In his efforts to show how close we were getting, Gable rolled his eyes and looked for all the world like Eddie Cantor.

'It's a poultice of some sort,' squeaked Lilli Palmer. Then we got it! From a dozen loyal throats Gable's team roared the words: 'Antiphlogistine poultice'. Victory was ours.

'How long, timekeeper?' But the man had seen enough. He was halfway back to New York with the awful diagnosis that movie stars, in his opinion, should still be in long clothes.

Try it, Trubshawe. Try it in the saloon bar, it's a thirsty game.

Yours ever

David

Niv and Trubshawe in the only film they made together, *The Pink Panther* (1964).

108

Art Upside Down

by David Niven

A letter to *The Times*, published 24 July 1973

Sir –

I write this not as a cynic – I honestly want to learn.

Twelve years ago, I had an urge to own a painting by Miró and I took the advice of Swiss friends, the possessors of outstanding collections. All were agreed upon two things:

(1) The intelligence of my urge, and

(2) The name of the best dealer in Switzerland.

I visited this man and he produced exactly what I thought I was looking for in size, colour, humour and movement. When he named the price, it was smelling salts time, but I am not the greatest actor in the world and the dealer took one look at my face and knew that he had made a sale.

Then he pressed his luck. 'The fascinating thing about this picture,' he said, 'is that when Miró finished it, like many other artists he turned it to the wall and didn't look at it again for six months. When he turned it round again he could not remember what he had been painting in the first place so he reversed it and finished it upside down! Isn't that amusing?'

Well, it was so amusing to me that my heart turned to stone. If the artist didn't know which way up his original idea should be, then I didn't want to

Niv, the would-be artist and art connoisseur.

109

fork out my hard earned cash to buy it.

The picture, needless to say, was snapped up by someone else and now is valued at ten times the original figure which makes my Scots blood boil. I console myself by feeling that my integrity is intact. Is it? I'd love to know.

David Niven
The Connaught Hotel, W1
19 July

To which letter *The Times* received these replies:

Sir – I am puzzled by Mr David Niven's letter. The Miró picture was the 'same size, colour, humour and movement' whichever way it was hung. Were he to grow tired of looking at it in one position, he could always stand on his head and look at it in reverse. My Scots blood, therefore, boils in sympathy with his, that, through a moment's thoughtlessness, he missed this double bargain.

George Malcolm Thomson
Garrick Club, WC2

Sir – A brief answer to Mr Niven's question is that Miró was a Surrealist and that one of Surrealism's most significant contributions to modern art was the notion that chance or accident can play an important and positive part in the process of creation.

Simon Wilson
Craven Mews, SW11

Sir – I would like to point out to Mr David Niven that it is obvious which way up my paintings should be hung – but nobody buys them.

Guy Francis
Sutton Coldfield, Warwickshire

A piece of artwork leaves David speechless in the film *The Impossible Years* (1968), with co-star Jeff Cooper.

Our Friend Niv

*Tributes from some of David Niven's
closest friends and associates*

John Mortimer

The Best Storyteller I Have Ever Known

WE MET EVERY two or three months, mostly when he was filming in England, and the purpose of these meetings was laughter. We would go to the Connaught Hotel, where David always stayed, and he would greet me with a cry of 'Fundador', a name I earned many years ago when we were working together in Spain on a movie only memorable to me now because it marked the beginning of a long and irreplaceable friendship. I suppose I then became unwisely addicted to Spanish brandy, so he called me 'Fundador' or 'Fundi' if in a particularly relaxed mood.

I those days he had a driver he called 'Yipes' because he alleged that the young Spaniard, if faced with two headlamps travelling towards him, would try to drive in between them, uttering a cry he must have learned from English comics. Nothing in the film was as entertaining as the drives to dinner, dicing with death on the road to Malaga.

He was simply the best storyteller I have ever known. He would begin quietly, almost throwing away the lines, his voice was soft and confidential and he seemed gently astonished by his misadventures, but he would eventually be overcome with the hilarity of his life and end up bubbling with laughter. Some of his stories became glorious set-pieces, such as the tale of the endless consequences of skiing downhill at a high speed with his zip undone ('I looked down and saw a small Eton blue acorn') or some of his

A delightful portrait of Niv taken in the mid-seventies.

115

early Hollywood reminiscences. And when we were together he would ransack my life for anecdotes, strange meetings and scarcely believable cases. David Niven was forever on the lookout for laughter. Luckily, the world has some of his stories in *The Moon's a Balloon*. What can't be recaptured is the charm, the sheer happiness of their delivery.

What can I remember? The days when he shared a house in Hollywood with Errol Flynn which they called 'Cirrhosis by the Sea', a place to which Niven once lured a girl on the pretext of being heartbreakingly lonely, and when she was finally persuaded, Flynn thundered at the door and shouted, 'Niven, you're making love in my bed *again*!' The time when he rode in *The Prisoner of Zenda* as Fritz von Tallenheim in a royal procession and his horse became, in mid-shot, amorously and inextricably involved with the horse on which Ronald Colman was riding.

If his stories were, perhaps, his greatest performances, he was still an impeccable film actor who could be, as he was in *Separate Tables*, enormously moving.

Above all he was a friend who always had time. He once came to lunch with us in the country and was found wandering the lanes, carrying the present he had bought, because he had arrived too early and was reluctant to knock at our door. Almost two years ago we had dinner together and I noticed a difficulty in his speech. Early this year I drove to visit him in Switzerland, he was very ill then and his voice was almost gone, but he was as funny and brave and welcoming as ever. 'Perhaps it's because I've talked too much in my life,' he whispered, 'that this has got me now.'

I've still got long, handwritten letters from him, but then came one typed by a secretary. 'My arm,' it said, 'seems to have gone over to the enemy.' On the Friday night when the news of his death came, we were getting ready to go to a party. I stood in the garden, unable to believe he would never walk the lanes round here again, waiting until he thought it polite to knock.

David Niven was an actor loved by an enormous public. His friends knew how much that love was merited.

Henley-on-Thames
August 1983

Tommy Phipps
The Silliest Idea I'd Ever Heard!

OVER A FIFTY-YEAR close relationship with David Niven there are many memories of the times we had together, most of them hilarious, a few, when we were young, mildly outrageous, all of them unforgettable.

During the past several years he came to New York infrequently.

His arrival was always announced the same way – a telephone call.

'Niv here. Lunch?'

My reaction to his visits was mixed – part delight, part horror – because lunch to David was never a couple of courses and a bit of a chat. It was four hours of glorious, hysterical laughter, barrels of wine, followed by the inevitable twenty-block walk 'to get a spot of health'.

I'll never forget our last walk together. It was up Madison Avenue when one of us said something that triggered a fit of giggles unlike any giggles any two people have ever had before. It was the full, hopeless hysteria.

I can see David now sitting on a fire hydrant, rocking back and forth, tears streaming down his cheeks, that unforgettable laugh rising higher and higher. I was in even worse shape, doubled up in a doorway – in deep pain.

I can remember the appalled looks of the passers-by. Here we were in the middle of the afternoon, two elderly men (one whose face seemed vaguely familiar) thrashing about, out of all control and, what was worse, obviously loving every minute of it.

This was the pattern of his visits and it lasted for however many days he was in New York.

By the time he left I was ruined: health gone, marriage in shreds, any pretence of being a senior citizen out of the window.

I'd just about got things back together when, once again, out of the blue, the dreaded call: 'Niv here. Lunch?'

There are many versions of how David and Hollywood came together – all of them amusing – suggesting that it was some sort of happenstance. If it was, I must have imagined an unforgettable chat he and I had together on the beach in Bermuda so many years ago. He was staying with me and we spent a good deal of time talking about our futures which, at that moment, were depressingly unsettled.

I clearly remember David suddenly grabbing my arm, swinging me around and me thinking I had never seen him so intense. He glanced around to make sure he couldn't be overheard then he leaned forward. 'Look, chum,' he whispered, 'I've had an idea, but you must swear on your life to keep it between us, because if it doesn't work I'm going to look bloody ridiculous.' And then he said the words I've never forgotten: 'I'm going out to Hollywood to try and be an actor.'

I clearly remember standing back and slowly looking him up and down. He was wearing bathing trunks; his enormous legs were bright red and beaten up from endless games of rugby and falling about on boats; his nose was peeling, he had a band-aid on his chin where he had cut himself shaving. And in that moment, in the boiling sun, what he had just suggested seemed just about the silliest idea I'd ever heard.

'You must be mad,' I said.

'Nutty as a fruit cake,' he said.

And then his eyes crinkled up as they always did when he really laughed hard, and in that instant I suddenly felt sorry for him.

Tommy Thighe

January 1984

118

Douglas Fairbanks Jnr

The Arrival of a Popular Young Man

I AM VERY flattered to contribute a little something to this book on my old friend David Niven. Even though most of my reminiscences would most probably be unprintable, perhaps I can rescue one or two that are suitable ...

Niv was a vastly amusing fellow, a 'gent' certainly, and one of the world's best companions and raconteurs who derived from a very fine 'upper middle-class' Scottish family and, like his brother, was originally a professional career soldier, having gone to Sandhurst and entered the Highland Light Infantry Regiment.

He had always been stagestruck and participated in many amateur theatrical productions as well as having had many friends among theatrical people and artists on both sides of the Atlantic.

We first met when he was living in a little cottage not far from my father's weekend house on the ocean. He was quite a popular young man about town, but had not yet made his mark. He had had a few odd jobs here and there in Hollywood.

Niv and I worked together when I did *The Prisoner of Zenda*. It was an all-star cast and he was very excited to be in it. He didn't have a very big part, but what he did with that very small part was quite remarkable. He just took what little there was and made much more of it than was on paper. It is hard to describe – but I am sure somebody else playing the same part would not

Niv with Douglas
Fairbanks Jnr and
three other famous
Hollywood stars,
Madeleine Carroll,
Ronald Colman
and C. Aubrey
Smith.

have been noticed. But Niv certainly was!

In his life he always seemed to be very self-assured – but often with people that is a cover-up for a great deal of insecurity underneath. I am not so certain about Niv – he so loved telling stories and recounting adventures and embroidering them and making them possibly funnier than they actually were, that he carried you along with him so you didn't really know what went on behind the poise, the wonderful, perpetual good humour and highly polished wit.

As to his illness, he knew there was no proper cure, so he decided to end his days bravely at his home in Switzerland with his wife and family. He preferred to die with style and dignity rather than end his days in some sad clinic or hospital.

Sincerely yours,

New York, October 1983

Lauren Bacall

He Was a True Life Enhancer

YES – HE SPARKLED.

Yes – he lit up every room he entered.

Yes – he was the best teller of stories I ever knew.

Yes – seeing him, the thought of seeing him, always brought a smile to my face and gave me a lift.

Oh, yes, he was a true life enhancer!

Over the more than thirty years we were friends – through all the laughter – David had the same fears that most actors have: that every job would be his last. But he never let that stop him. When movies were in transition and offers not pouring in, he moved into television and did it better than anyone. He wrote books, witty, bestselling books. He loved his home, his family, his friends. He had a zest for life.

But what loomed largest was his great capacity for love and friendship – his gift for laughter.

For my part, when Bogie was ill he was right there – all the time – any time. When Bogie died he was right there all the time. And the words he spoke to me one night about dealing with loss were the words I remembered most clearly all the nights and years afterward. They were the words that gave me strength when I needed it.

And, oh, the man had personal courage – never proven more clearly than during his own illness.

David Niven was rare – a man to be treasured – of immeasurable value. An original. I shall never stop missing him or remembering him.

St Louis, December 1983

Dame Flora Robson
Our First Meeting in Hollywood

My FIRST HOLLYWOOD film was *Wuthering Heights* made in 1939 in which I appeared as the housekeeper, Ellen Dean. Also in the picture were Laurence Olivier and David Niven who was then just getting his career under way, I remember.

I find in my scrapbook that he had some rather nice things to say about our working together. 'When I was a total beginner in *Wuthering Heights* she was charming to me when she could have been horrid,' he says, 'and ever since then in the pictures we have shared together she had always been a joy to be with.'

David may have felt a total beginner, but Laurence Olivier and I were also made to feel pretty unimportant to start with. When I arrived walking at the studio for the first morning's work I was promptly turned away by the guard. However, I managed to get in by a side door marked 'Entrance for Extras'.

When I reached the set of *Wuthering Heights*, I was on the point of bursting into tears and could only ask, 'Please give me a card of admission. The people on the gate threw me out!'

A short time later I met Laurence Olivier who had also been brought out from England, and he told me he had received exactly the same treatment. The Americans apparently could not believe anyone starring in a movie would *walk* to the studios!

Twenty years later when David Niven was himself a star we made *55 Days in Peking*. He played the British envoy and I was the Dowager Empress. We were together again in *Eye of the Devil* in 1966 and also had a most amusing reunion in *The Canterville Ghost* eight years after when David played the ghost! Our last picture together was the war drama, *A Man Called Intrepid*, in which I played a nun, Sister Luke.

I always enjoyed acting with David Niven. He was so warm-hearted, and I *never* heard him ever say anything unkind about his colleagues.

The famous bedside scene in *Wuthering Heights* with Laurence Olivier and Flora Robson.

Flora Robson

Brighton, October 1983

125

Lord Olivier

Never a Fair-Weather Friend

Perhaps a little surprisingly, on
account of his perennial jolly-good-fellow
sort of greeting, with his sideways nod to
all and sundry, whether it was the electricians
on the gantries or his very best chum, one
apprehended entirely wrongly that his affections
were not perhaps of the greatest depth in the
records of human relations - in other words
that he was a "fair weather friend."

But in truth I know this to be an
entirely false impression and that David
was the dearest, the kindest, the most
giving and the most inspiringly faithful
friend that anyone could take pride in
possessing.

Laurence Olivier

Laurence Olivier

The Rt Hon.
Lord Hailsham

On Duty with David Niven

DAVID NIVEN WAS not well known to me, and our contacts were few. But it would not be too much to say that we were friends.

As recounted in his autobiography, there was a brief period in the Second World War during which we worked together in the same office wearing the uniform of the same regiment. More than that, when I was a platoon officer in Lincolnshire, nearly all the new members of the platoon recounted how they had served in his platoon at the depot. He was evidently immensely popular with them and not only because of his fame.

Readers of *The Moon's a Balloon* will remember the poignant story of the accident which befell his first wife, Primmie. Perhaps it was this which led him after many years to write the most generous and touching letter to me when I was stricken with a similar misfortune.

I wrote to him twice during his last illness and received, by a third hand, a gracious acknowledgement of our friendship.

Hailsham

House of Lords
October 1983

127

Phil Gersh
Agent

Starring Around the World

PRIOR TO DAVID becoming 'a superstar, he was frustrated because it was difficult to obtain the leading roles in important films such as *Around the World in Eighty Days*.

David was most eager to play the leading role of a Victorian gentleman in the Mike Todd production of the Jules Verne classic. However, Mike wanted Cary Grant for this role, and Cary was under contract to MGM at the time. Mike decided that he would wait and take his chances that perhaps Cary would become available.

During this period of approximately six months, I had to arrange for three separate meetings with Mike Todd and each time David had to express his enthusiasm for the role and literally plead with Mike. Fortunately for David, Mike Todd had a starting date for the production and Cary Grant was still unavailable. This role was *the* turning point in David's career.

Subsequent to the success of *Around the World in Eighty Days*, David played another great role in an important film entitled *Separate Tables* for which he won an Academy Award.

However, prior to the release of *Separate Tables*, David and I had lunch at Romanoff's and at this time he did not have a future commitment. During the lunch, David turned to me and sort of whispered, 'Nobody wants me. I guess I'm finished and perhaps I should return to London where I feel there is employment.'

Of course, you know the rest of the story.

Sincerely,

Phil Gersh

Beverly Hills
California
October 1983

Overleaf:
Discussing
*Around the World
in Eighty Days*
with producer,
Mike Todd.

Sir John Mills, CBE

The Actor Who Never Got Egg On His Face

THE PART WHICH put David Niven right back at the top of the tree, Phileas Fogg in *Around the World in Eighty Days*, was also the only film in which Niv and I both appeared although we were friends for a great many years. And even then, due to the wonders of film technology, we never even laid eyes on one another while it was being made! Making the film also proved to be almost as tough as Fogg's original journey, but it all paid off in the end.

I think Niv was one of the only actors I've known who could appear in a really pretty ghastly film and somehow be the only one who emerged at the end without egg all over his face – and that is a very great gift. If he had any regrets at all as an actor – and I don't think there were many – one minor gripe was that he didn't get to play villains as often as he would have liked. A few more rogues like Raffles in his gallery would have been very welcome.

Writing, I think, gave Niv even more pleasure than acting, though he found it, he said, absolute torture. When I was sweating over my own autobiography, I telephoned Niv and asked him for his advice. He said, 'Well, I'll tell you what to do. I take a lot of children's exercise books, plenty of sharpened pencils and a rubber. I write all through the morning, have half a bottle of Beaujolais for lunch, and rub it all out in the afternoon.'

The thing I remember most about David Niven was his immense capacity for laughter. He also had the most enormous personal courage right up to the last.

John Mills with Clifton James, the man David Niven trained to play the part of Monty's 'Double'. A still from *I Was Monty's Double*.

The last letter I received from him, when he could only just write, said, 'I'm clobbered with this ridiculous disease. The doctors seem very confused by it, but I have, at last, found the right man. He has put me on a cure which is splendid and I have no doubt will do the trick. It is quite simple, I merely drink half a pint of Drambuie mixed with half a pint of asses' milk every morning before breakfast. I am finding it terrific!'

I had known David for the last forty-odd years and I cannot remember one occasion which was not full of laughter. There will never be another David Niven.

London, November 1983

Deborah Kerr

Memories of My Dear Old Chum

I AM SO happy to hear that a book is to be published about my 'dear old chum' as he always called me. Our platonic relationship had endured for forty years – sometimes years passed without our communicating and suddenly I will have written *to* him and received a letter *from* him the next day.

This also happened with the telephone – I would say to myself: 'My God, I must call Niv' and the phone would ring and it would be him! We used to call it 'telepathers'!

I was also called by both David and Hjordis, his wife, 'Hil' – short for Hilda – a Cockney charlady I used to pretend to be, who came and 'did' for Mr and Mrs Niven during the season at Chateau d'Oex! It was a game we played and always found hilarious!

We made five films together, and both of us having the same juvenile sense of humour we would break each other up to such an extent that tears of suppressed laughter were pouring down our faces. This may seem rather inconsequential, but I think illustrates his extraordinary facility for turning the most trivial happening into a running joke.

As a raconteur he was unsurpassed, and his eye and ear for capturing whoever he was writing about, infallible. His letters were always written in film-type dialogue, and reduced me to hysterical laughter. His humour was boundless and his charm and warmth to everyone made him deeply loved. What a fabulous contribution his life made to us all!

It was so ironical that his illness was such a terrible one. Even in his letters towards the end he would joke about it. In his last handwritten letter, he said: '... dear old chum, don't stretch the elastic too far, because it snaps, and that is what has happened to me.' He was referring to his continuous work, and he knew I too had been working non-stop in the theatre.

I do not know if any of this will be of use to you. But I hope so, because I would hate a book to be published without some expression of my fondness and gratitude for his friendship over the years, through thick and thin. I know he would not want us to mourn. He would prefer us to 'have a beaker old chum'. He was indeed 'The Last Gentleman'.

Deborah Kerr

Malaga, Spain
October 1983

Niv and his 'old chum' in arguably the most famous film scene of his career from *Separate Tables*.

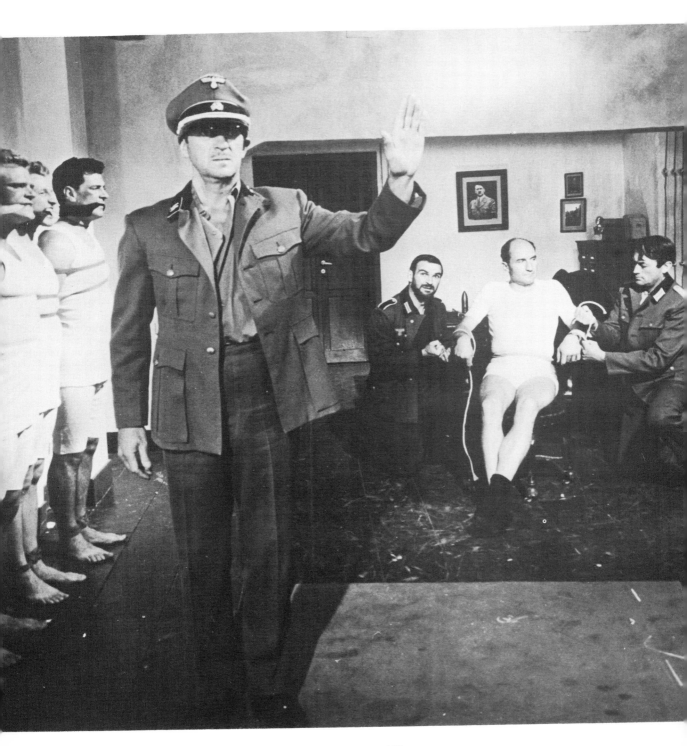

Jerome Chodorov
Screenwriter

The Man Who Set His Own Fashions

THE TROUBLE IS, of course, that David had all the best stories and, what's more, he published them. Anything he told me he's used – and to much better effect than I could. Like everyone else, though, I was charmed by him.

But I did get the feeling that underneath all his gaiety and loving good will was another Niven, a man who disguised his true feelings much of the time. Perhaps all that is some Freudian brainwashing of my own, but I don't think so. Am I the only one who detected a distant wondering look in his eyes from time to time?

Anyway, the one delightful thing I doubt anyone else has brought up is the fact that David made no concessions to men's fashions at all. At least not in the fifties when we lunched almost every day making *Happy Anniversary*.

You remember when lapels went from wide to narrow, and ties from narrow to wide and back again (I think they're still doing it, but out here we never wear ties) and suits were form-fitting and then loose? Well, David had a beautiful wardrobe of old expensive suits with narrow waists and wide lapels, and he wasn't about to drop *any* of them.

His attitude was 'what I wear *is* the style'. And, by God, it was! He looked better than anyone else.

A 'stylish' Niven? A scene from *The Guns of Navarone* (1961) in which he co-starred with Stanley Baker and Gregory Peck.

Beverly Hills
October 1983

Lana Turner

I Truly Adored That Gentle Man

December 30, 1983

Mr Peter Haining
Editor
WH Allen & Co. Ltd.
44 Hill Street
London, England
WiX8LB

Dear Mr. Haining,

The following is my contribution to
the book you are doing on David Niven:

MY MEMORY OF DAVID IS THAT NO MATTER
WHERE OR WHEN WE MET THERE WAS AN AURA
OF LIGHTNESS AND HAPPINESS AROUND HIM.
WHEN I THINK OF DAVID I ALWAYS SMILE.
I TRULY ADORED THAT GENTLE MAN.

My best wishes to you and your worthy
project.

Sincerely,

Lana Turner

Brian Doyle
Film publicity director

Did I Ever Tell You About the Time ...

DAVID NIVEN WAS very special and I found it a joy and delight to work with him. I only regret that I was associated with him on only two films: *Vampira*, in 1973 (in which he portrayed what must have been the most charming Count Dracula ever to have been immortalised on celluloid), and *The Sea Wolves*, in 1979–80, in which he played Colonel of the Calcutta Light Horse, a territorial unit in India, which carried out a spectacular secret operation during World War II.

One of my jobs as Publicity Director was to arrange press interviews and David was naturally professional enough to know that such interviews with the media are part-and-parcel of being a movie star. 'I'll leave it to you, old boy,' he would say, 'if you think he (or she) is a nice, reasonably intelligent journalist and that whatever they write for is worthwhile, then I'll do it.' And do it he did, fitting in interviews between shooting and rehearsals and camera set-ups, without fuss or bother (but *never* at lunchtimes – they were sacrosanct to his 'salad and snooze').

He usually liked me to 'sit in' on interviews for several reasons, one being that I could 'rescue' him if the interview went on for too long, or occasionally if he found the journalist 'boring'. We worked out a system in the latter case, in which he would tug at his ear and look at me if he wanted the meeting to be brought swiftly but politely to a close!

I was a willing 'sitter-in' on all those press interviews. David loved talking. And people enjoyed listening to him. He was without doubt one of the best, if not *the* best, raconteurs in show business, as well as being one of the most popular and best-loved. My face often ached with laughter after one of his colourful sessions of anecdotes and reminiscences.

He was something of a practical joker too. During one sequence in *Vampira*, Count Dracula turns black. So, with the aid of make-up, did David. We were filming in London's West End, and a car dropped him off, at the end of work, at the Connaught Hotel, where he always preferred to stay when in London.

What happened next became one of David's favourite (and perhaps apocryphal?) stories. According to him, he walked up to the reception desk, still in his black make-up and wearing a black cloak and large black hat, and, in a deep Southern American voice, asked for his key. What key would that be, asked a suspicious clerk. Mr Niven's key – Mr Niven had said he could borrow his suite while he was in town on vacation, said the dark stranger. The clerk refused to hand the key over and the manager was called. Voices were raised and the police were about to be called when the dark figure collapsed with laughter and revealed his identity to an astonished hotel staff.

David would act out this story, adding hilarious embellishments with each telling, and it was very funny. Sceptical listeners would say that surely the hotel staff *must* have recognised the unmistakable Niven? At this point, David would appeal to me. 'Ask Brian – he was there and saw it all – didn't you, old boy?' 'Oh, yes ... absolutely, yes, David, quite right ...' I would stammer. I hadn't been present on that classic occasion, but who would dare spoil such a good story?

I suppose I came to know David Niven best during the three months shooting on *The Sea Wolves*, in late-1979 and early-1980, in India, where the fine cast also included old friends of David's such as Gregory Peck, Roger Moore and Trevor Howard, as well as producer Euan Lloyd.

Frequently, after finishing a scene, he would put his arm around my shoulder and say 'Come along, old friend, let's go for a stroll. Did I ever tell you about the time when ...' And then I would be treated to a string of wonderful anecdotes.

When I took him to do an interview for Indian TV in New Delhi ('Delly Telly' as he dubbed it), the producer presented him with a neck-tie of such violent hues (yellow and orange predominated, I recall) that the eyes grew dizzy. In the car on the way back to the hotel, he said he would like me to have it, but that I must wear it that evening at dinner. With well-founded misgivings I did so, only to have David constantly berating my choice of ties and saying 'My God, whatever possessed you to wear that terrible tie, Brian? You have no taste at all, I'm surprised at you, old boy ...!'

He heartily disliked what he called 'boring people' and 'boring occasions'. In India, a group of us once attended a small lunch-party given by some Government VIP. David was not in his usual high spirits, since he had just learned of the death of his old friend, actress Merle Oberon. He was anxious to leave soon after he had arrived and pronounced the lunch 'a frightful bore' to me in a stage whisper that had me glancing over my shoulder in case anyone had heard. When the time eventually came for our party to depart, I stood behind David as he said goodbye to our hostess. 'Thank you so much, I've had a really horrible time and I can't wait to get away,' he said in a very low voice. His intention was that the august hostess could not catch exactly what he had said and I don't think she did. But I did!

David had a fear of growing old and made no secret of it. And he didn't

Niv's most unusual role? As Count Dracula in *Vampira* made in 1973.

like people knowing his age. In India, he happened to read a copy of a biography I had written of him for press use, and insisted that I delete his birthdate. 'But it's in all the reference books, David,' I protested. 'Let them look up the books then, there's no need to broadcast exactly how old I am in our hand-outs,' he said.

The last time I saw him, we sat in his caravan in Goa, India, during the last week's work on *The Sea Wolves*. He was writing his last book, a novel, in ballpoint pen in exercise-books. 'I'm stuck in the middle of a sexy love-scene — me!' he sighed. He said he found writing very hard work and, though

With a host of 'chums' while making *The Sea Wolves* in 1980.

such glorious books as *The Moon's a Balloon* and *Bring On the Empty Horses* read so easily, they were the result of much sweat and labour. 'I get so easily distracted when I'm writing,' he told me, 'that at home I sit facing a blank wall so that nothing takes my concentration away. Until I start thinking about blank walls!'

He pushed his writing away and looked at me seriously for once. 'You know, Brian, I'm terrified,' he said. 'Why?' I asked in surprise. 'I'll be seventy next month – *seventy!* I feel fine now, thank God, but old age has got to start creeping on one day soon. And, frankly, I'm scared. I don't want to be old. I've always felt so young. And I want to *stay* young.' Then he grinned and said 'Well, I mustn't get too maudlin, that would never do. Did I ever tell you about the time ...'

When David became ill and went to London for special treatment, I wrote to him. I didn't really expect a reply. He had other things to think about. Several weeks later, he sent me a handwritten letter from his home at Cap Ferrat. It was cheerful and jokey and at one point he said 'Don't ever get a serious illness, old boy – it's such a total waste of time.' He ended 'See you sometime soon, I hope, your old friend, David.' A month later he was dead.

David Niven was a motion picture star for over forty years and knew practically every star, producer and director in the business. And he was liked and respected by ninety-nine per cent of them. Someone once asked him why he was so well-liked by everyone.

'I suppose it's really because I *like* to be liked by everyone,' he replied simply. 'I like most people and, if people sense that you like them, then they like you too. Just imagine if everyone was like that – there'd be no wars or fights or arguments at all. Everyone would be far too busy liking everyone else!'

David Niven. The name is enough. Everyone knew him, either personally, or vicariously through his films or books or media interviews. And everyone liked him.

There'll never be another David Niven.

Brian Doyle

London, December 1983

Bette Davis

A Joy Never to be Forgotten

$\mathcal{BD}$

December 15, 1983

Dear Mr. Haining,

David Niven was indeed a
gentleman but not the last gentleman
in films. Another very much alive
gentleman is James Stewart. Being
of an optimistic nature I am sure
there are many more to come as the
years go by.

I made one film with David
Niven "Death On the Nile". He was
a joy to work with. It is indeed a
tragedy that he is gone. Thanks to the
frequency of motion pictures on television,
even though he has left us, he will not
be forgotten as we will see his many
fine performances very often on television.

Bette Davis

Niv reunited with
his former
batman, Peter
Ustinov, and
Bette Davis on
the set of *Murder
on the Nile*
(1978).

147

Greg Bautzer

Lawyer

The Case of Niven, Howard Hughes and some Beautiful Ladies ...

I WAS PRIVILEGED (perhaps blessed is a better word) to have known David Niven most of my adult life, and I admired his immense talents as an actor and writer as well as his compassionate consideration as a human being.

One of my recollections concerning him was in connection with Howard Hughes who at the time owned RKO Studios. Hughes was, unfortunately, competing with Darryl Zanuck at Twentieth Century-Fox for Niven's services and simultaneously competing with David in the quest for several beautiful ladies.

David had a great presence and wonderful charm and that was one of the reasons he was adored by women. One day I was having a meeting with Howard Hughes when the subject of Niven came up because David was seeing a young lady that Hughes had an interest in. A very beautiful and talented young actress from Hollywood – but she preferred Niven's company, much to Mr Hughes' chagrin. So we were talking about Niven and he said, 'What is it about this man?'

'Howard, he's not only got great ability, he is a wonderful human being,' I said.

'Well, he sure must have something because most of the women in town are crazy about him.'

'Well, he is equally liked by men,' I added.

The ageless charmer – Niv as Sir James Bond in *Casino Royale* (1967).

148

'I am having a terrible time with this young lady. The only time I get to see her is when Niven is busy! It must be wonderful to be someone like David, because when a woman goes to bed with him she is going to bed with *him* and not his money,' Howard exclaimed.

'There is a solution,' I declared. 'Why don't you give all your money to charity,' to which he replied:

'But then no one would go to bed with me!'

It is true to say that David Niven was very well regarded by both the producers in the studios – as well as his peers in the profession – as a very able actor. And the success that he had as an actor is testimony to that fact. He was also highly regarded by people in general because he was a giver rather than a taker.

A problem with many actors is that they are so self-centred that they become ego-maniacs, but not so with David.

There are very few gallant men – particularly in our profession – but if one word could sum up David Niven, it is that he was a *gallant* man.

Los Angeles
January 1984

Gregory Peck

A Gallant and High-Spirited Journey

TWENTY YEARS AGO this past summer, David had a picture to make in Hollywood, and I had one to make in Switzerland, so we agreed on a house swap. It was a nice arrangement ... our house in Brentwood for his chalet in Chateau d'Oex.

I've been looking through our 1963 correspondence, and I found this from David. 'We have been very chic, Hjordis and I. The President and Madame, who were old friends, (but whom we have not seen since they "moved",) invited us to come to Washington for a family party on the yacht on the President's Birthday. It was the greatest possible relaxed fun. Dom Perignon was aboard too, and we got back to the dock at 3.30 A.M.

'We really had a marvellous time, and were incidentally deeply impressed.

'The next day, Memorial Day, we spent up at Camp David, just the four of us.

'No matter what anybody votes, a most exceptionally brilliant man is running the country. He also has the wonderful gift that Churchill had ... he can switch off the worries and either enjoy himself ... or go straight to sleep.'

I have an idea that JFK and Jackie Kennedy had an even more marvellous time ... because there simply was no one else, as far as I know, as brilliantly entertaining, funny and captivating as David in full form. The Kennedys,

Overleaf: Niv with three of his closest 'chums': Trevor Howard, Gregory Peck and Roger Moore, in a typical Niven set-up.

151

and all of David's pals, were the *lucky* ones ... all of us were who shared, in some measure, David's gallant and high-spirited journey.

And what a journey! What a terrific run David had, touching all the bases. What enjoyment and pleasure he brought to his friends, and to the millions who watched him on the screen.

The beginnings of his life were somewhat Dickensian. A father who was killed in combat in the Great War, when David was five – a beautiful mother who had to struggle to make ends meet, a dubious stepfather, various boarding schools, some good, and not so good. As a small boy, there was loneliness and uncertainty, the usual canings, expulsion from one of the good schools for a very funny, somewhat Rabelasian prank – all culminating, however, in academic success at Stowe, consequent acceptance at Sandhurst, and, on graduation, a commission in the Army.

Typically, David, asked to name, in order of preference, three regiments in which he would like to be commissioned, wrote:

1. The Argyle and Sutherland Highlanders
2. The Black Watch
3. *Anything* but the Highland Light Infantry.

He was commissioned in the Highland Light Infantry.

He served in Malta, and in England, and then after his first trip to New York while on leave, decided there was no great future in the Army for a young man of limited means. He resigned his commission and made his way back to New York, where he landed on his feet with his famous job as a liquor salesman for Club 21.

Within a year he was in Hollywood. His first job was as a Mexican extra. For that he was painted every morning with a brown mixture from a spray gun – but before long he was hob-nobbing with the likes of Douglas Fairbanks, Darryl Zanuck, Irving Thalberg – and signed to a seven-year contract with Sam Goldwyn. He wasn't any good at first – he was 'ghastly and gibbering with fright', (his own words), but he learned, with the help of friends, and some great directors like Eddie Goulding, Ernst Lubitsch and Willy Wyler.

David became a star during the Goldern Era of the thirties. His friends – the people he worked with and had fun with were Clark Gable, Cary Grant, Errol Flynn, Spencer Tracy, Humphrey Bogart, Tyrone Power, Loretta Young, Merle Oberon, Jean Harlow, Norma Shearer, Joan Crawford, Myrna Loy, Claudette Colbert, Fred Astaire, Ginger Rogers to name a few. It was a glittering decade in Hollywood, the thirties, and David loved every minute of it.

We know the continuity of David's life. Distinguished service in the British Army in World War II, marriage to Primmie, his pride in his two fine sons, the shocking loss of Primmie – and eventually a new chapter, marriage to Hjordis, two little girls whom he adored, and the life in Switzerland and Cap Ferrat.

The career flourished, with a few dry spells. Early pictures were *Wuthering Heights* and *Dodsworth*. Outstanding successes along the way were *The Moon is Blue* and *The Guns of Navarone*. Especially memorable were *Around the World in Eighty Days*, and *Separate Tables*, his Academy Award-winning picture. With time out for the War, David was an international star from the mid-thirties until the early eighties – almost fifty years.

It was truly a great run. David's success as an author, with *The Moon's a Balloon*, and *Bring On the Empty Horses* gave him a great deal of satisfaction. Bill Buckley wrote this: 'David Niven is known among his friends as, quite simply, an incomparable companion. Always, when asked why, they were never able to communicate his particular magic. Now all we have to do is say: Read his book. It's all there.'

Three years ago, David, Roger Moore, Trevor Howard and I were in India, working. David was chipper as always. He didn't much like his part, but he made it look a lot better than it was. That was what he was paid to do. The thing was that he'd begun, religiously, to take long, fast walks every day, late in the afternoon, after work. There was a good place for it, a beach ten miles long, at Goa, on the Indian ocean, where we were filming. He had begun his valiant fight, his refusal to accept muscular weakness, and it was to last for three years. Never has a man fought a losing battle with such courage and such an outrageous sense of humour about the thing that was to bring an end to his life – the life that had been lived with such vigour, with such a manly appetite for everything that was beautiful, excellent, graceful, funny, with such thoughtfulness for his friends, such a rare sensitivity to the feelings of others, such a love of family, such pride in his talented and successful sons.

It was a triumphant life in terms of what David achieved, in what he did as an actor and writer, and what he was as a father, friend, as a man. For decades, David's friends and people in general who knew him only from his work, had a way of breaking into a smile, in a good way, a warm way, whenever his name came up. He was fun to know; he was a gentleman, a gentle knight, the 'very pink of courtesy'. He was chivalrous, affable, intensely human, unfailingly kind. In the end, in the face of the inevitable, he made fun of it. Is there greater courage? Could a man leave a richer legacy to his children and his friends? Here are a few things he said to me in letters during the past year: I had suggested that he try Ginseng root, of a special sort, from the mountains of mainland China, procurable through Hong Kong. This is what he said: 'Apart from all the great specialists, I have made the rounds of faith healers and quacks, the last being a vineyard worker near Sion with hands like bunches of bananas. He ripped up my records from the Mayo Clinic with a happy laugh and told me that all would be well if I bathed three times a day in olive oil and brandy! Anyway, I'm pressing on, and let's face it, millions of people have worse things than mine.'

David loved Cap Ferrat. He wrote about it last April after one of his walks. 'It was a glorious evening. A rainstorm had been blown away by the Mistral and from the top by the lighthouse I could see the big hills behind St Tropez in one direction and great chunks of the Italian Coast in the other. The sea was deep, deep blue, and there was snow on the mountains behind Nice.'

Here was his last note: 'Caro Fagiolo Vecchio,' (Dear Old Bean) 'Just a scrawl to thank you once more for the Ginseng and other very kind thoughts. Sadly that wonder root arrived too late to reverse my miserable disease – and I was ten days in hospital being fed like a Strasbourg goose to try and regain ten lost kilos. Please give a big kiss to Veronique. Much love, dear friend.'

We should not mourn David. He wouldn't care for mourning. I think we should celebrate a life that was well and truly lived, and so we can say the same thing to him – Much love, dear friend.

Beverly Hills
California
October 1983

Gene Kelly

A Man Who Could Brighten a Whole Room

October 10, 1983

Yes, David Niven was a wit,
raconteur and a gifted actor,
but to all of us who knew him,
he was much more than that.
He was one of those rare people
of the world who would enter a
room and the whole room would
brighten up.

Now many fine artists are
excellent at their crafts and
bring joy to the public who
watches them. But David not
only did that, as the whole
world knows, but in his personal
contacts brought joy and a sense
of good fellowship to all those
around him.

He will be greatly missed.

Gene Kelly

Bryan Forbes

Niv's Life was a Marvellous Party

'WHAT WAS IT about David Niven?' somebody asked me as the news of his untimely death circulated like a bushfire of sorrow, engulfing friends and strangers alike. Perhaps the truth of the matter is he had been so universally liked and enjoyed for so long that he was not so much a star but more a way of life. Perhaps the secret of the great affection he inspired in colleagues and fans was that, in a world that has changed too quickly, he pushed out a lot of happiness to others and in so doing reminded them of better days.

Doubtless many of the obituaries will draw attention to his reputation as a quintessential Englishman – a touch of the man who broke the bank at Monte Carlo, the understated war hero so beloved by film-makers, the sauve, impeccably-dressed *bon viveur*. But this is by no means the whole picture.

I knew him as somebody always genuinely surprised that he had survived in a profession not noted for its critical charity. He was a truly funny man, never more content than when he was out of the limelight, surrounded by chums and enjoying his own more often than not unprintable anecdotes.

He had few of the conceits usually associated with a star of his calibre, and although he deliberately gave the impression that he was nothing more than a lucky actor who happened to be around at the right time, he was, in fact, the complete professional.

He was, disarmingly, amazed by the success of his books. 'Good loo reading,' he would say. 'I'm not a real writer, just a dabbler.' But there he was wrong, for trapped within the pages of his hilarious volumes of autobiography was the distilled, unadulterated essence of a man who wrote without fear or favour to himself, who wrote as he talked and acted in real life.

One of his greatest talents was his genius for self-mockery. He was never funnier than when relating a story against himself and, although I am sure that over the years some of these became heavily embroidered, they always aged in the wood.

When Roger Moore and I saw him for the last time a few weeks before his

One of Bryan Forbes' own photographs of Niv and Art Carney working on what was to be his last starring role in *Better Late Than Never* (1981).

death, he insisted on making the painful journey from his sick-room to greet us upright – still elegant, still making light of what in his heart he must have known was a terminal condition, still avid for the latest gossip, for news of old chums. The only chink in his armour he allowed us to see was his frustration at being unable to articulate his side of the story, since the illness which finally took his life was the cruellest that can befall an actor, for it deprived him of his voice – the inimitable instrument by which an actor lives.

When we talk of past giants in our profession, we are often denied visible evidence of their talents, but where David is concerned we are more fortunate. We have, preserved at twenty-four frames per second, so many different aspects of his unique career. And we also have his books. Taken together they show him in the round and the combined portrait is a true one, warts and all.

He also had the great gift of making women of all ages feel that they were the only person in the room – something which both our daughters can attest to, for even as small children he always treated them as *femmes fatales*, which they found irresistible.

He first came to fame during the great heyday of the Hollywood studio system, and it was a characteristic of that vanished world that, once they had set an actor in a mould, they never broke it. Thus it was David's transient misfortune to be typecast in a series of roles. It was not until he rejoined the British Army as a volunteer at the outbreak of the last war that he truly came into his own and was able to demonstrate hitherto unsuspected depths to his talent. And when finally he gained the role in the film version of Rattigan's *Separate Tables*, he grasped the nettle with both hands and went on to win an Academy Award.

On the set he was devoid of boring displays of temperament that so often disguise a lack of talent. He was easy-going as always, but had the discipline of somebody brought up in the old, tough school of pre-war Hollywood. He was a compulsive worker, always prepared to believe that his long run of luck was about to end. I have a suspicion that this recurrent fear, so characteristic of many actors, hastened his end.

The day after we finished shooting *Ménage à Trois* in the South of France, he took off for a gruelling, whistlestop tour of the United States to promote his latest novel. During this trip his health, which he had pushed too far, began to deteriorate. But that, I am sure, was the way he wanted it.

I shall think back to the long weeks we spent together on that film with a feeling of privilege – for, although we had been friends for three decades, this was the first time we had worked together. I wrote a role for him which he professed to like: that of a broken-down cabaret artist singing Noel Coward songs to uncomprehending German tourists in a Juan les Pins strip joint. The song we chose was 'I've Been to a Marvellous Party' and in so many ways this epitomises my fondest memories of him.

To be with the dear old Niv was to be at an endless, marvellous party, and it is entirely typical that his last gesture was a thumbs-up sign – though with his irreverent sense of humour which never deserted him, it is highly probable that he really intended a more profane wave goodbye, employing two fingers.

Virginia Water, Surrey
August 1983

George Greenfield
Literary agent

Taking a Ride to the Stars

HE WANTED TO write a book – but what kind of book? He decided to seek advice from an old friend, a fellow member of White's, who happened to be a successful publisher. 'Whatever you do, David', said his friend, 'never, never write a book about Hollywood.' (Two years after *The Moon's a Balloon* had become an extraordinary international success – with sales already more than five million worldwide – the same publishing friend wrote to the author with more advice. 'Never, never write *another* book about Hollywood'.)

There had been an earlier book, *Round the Ragged Rocks*, which was a fictional version of Niven's own story. It had been published by Cresset Press in the fifties, had done moderately well and had gone out of print. Once *Moon* had burst on the scene, Niven would never discuss the previous work and would not allow it to be reprinted, although there were numerous requests from British and American publishers. He once said that re-reading it was like watching one of his early, callow attempts at film-acting.

Looking back on the enormous success that *The Moon's a Balloon* achieved, it is easy to assume that everything was plain sailing, that the debonair actor just sat down with a glass of champagne and dictated the book in spare moments when he was off-screen and that the book on publication just floated smoothly aloft like the balloon in the title. The truth

was quite different. David Niven was a professional in everything he did; he wrote in a large copperplate hand – but there were few lines and no paragraphs that did not contain crossings-out and new words substituted. He welcomed criticism – indeed, he was probably too receptive to amateur critics. He once altered a brilliant line because a chambermaid at The

Niv, the great storyteller, entertaining the late Peter Sellers and Claudia Cardinale.

Connaught, to whom he had read the passage, did not understand a certain word. It took a great deal of arguing on the part of his publisher and editor to get him to go back to the original draft.

Nor was the selling of *The Moon's a Balloon* a pushover. When his British publishers, Hamish Hamilton, came to sell paperback rights, every reprint house but one, Coronet Books, flatly rejected the offer. (Pan Books did half-heartedly suggest £500 if the author would tear out the second half of the story and just concentrate on his early days, but that proposal was treated with the contempt it deserved.)

Coronet was persuaded to raise its offer to an advance of £750 but would not budge a penny higher. So reluctantly David agreed to accept the offer. Clearly, paperback publishers felt that few of their readers would be interested in the memoirs of an actor who had never been in the very first flight of star names.

The Moon's a Balloon was highly successful in its British hardcover edition, selling well over 100,000 copies. But it was a riotous success as a paperback. Within days, it seemed, sales rocketed over the million mark – and then over the two million figure and eventually to well over three million. The book that had been almost universally spurned by the paperback trade had become one of the best sellers of all time.

A very charming and generous gesture occurred on the way to the stars. Soon after sales had passed the first million, Philip Evans, the then Editorial Director of Coronet, telephoned me. He said that he was embarrassed at the modest terms on which they had bought the book. The advance had long since been earned out – but he felt that Coronet should retrospectively improve the royalty rates by a substantial degree. David Niven was touched by the voluntary offer and gladly accepted. Not long afterwards, Philip Evans had a serious car accident and for several years was confined to a wheelchair at his home in West London. Whenever David visited London and no matter how busy he might be with the many appointments he fitted into his brief stay, he always found time to slip across to Philip's home and spend an hour or two with him.

If *The Moon's a Balloon* had a chequered initial career in England, that was nothing compared to its early reception in New York. Buoyed up by my enthusiasm for the book, I decided to auction the American rights and, to separate the men from the boys, set a reserve price of $35,000. I swept into New York, lugging eight copies of the pretty thick script with me. My first appointment – shrewdly chosen, I thought – was with Michael Korda at Simon & Schuster. As the nephew of Sir Alexander Korda for whom Niven had made several films, he would surely be the man to approve the book's qualities.

I plonked the heavy script on his desk and said my piece. In a gesture reminiscent (to older moviegoers) of that scene in *The Informer*, where the British officer pushes the betrayal money to Victor Maclaglan with his swagger stick, Michael prodded the script towards me with the backs of his knuckles. 'Take it away,' he said. 'He's an ageing, ham British actor – take it away.'

I urged him at least to read the first fifty pages. 'I wouldn't read the first five pages,' he answered. 'No one over here is interested in Niven.'

I retorted that he had been promised appearances on the 'Today Show', the 'Johnny Carson Show' and the 'Merv Griffin Show'. 'That's what they all say,' Michael said wearily. 'It never happens.'

A few months later, Pocket Books, which is the associated paperback house of Simon & Schuster, offered $350,000 for the reprint rights in *Moon* but were overbid elsewhere. If Michael Korda had bought the rights, when first offered, at a tenth of that sum, Pocket Books could have had reprint rights for nothing. But the later thought of Michael's discomfiture was no consolation as I trudged away from his office with the heavy script under one arm.

The auction was a flop. Of the eight publishers involved, four refused to bid at all, two came up with $10,000, one with $16,000 and the top bidder with $20,000. This was John Dodds, then at Putnam. I managed to persuade him to increase his offer to $22,500 – and then had to do a major job of persuasion with my unhappy author, who with good logic thought we should withdraw the book as it had failed to reach its reserve price. Finally and reluctantly, he agreed – and within months *Moon* had repeated its British success, Putnam selling over 150,000 copies in their hardcover edition and Dell upwards of a million and a half in the paperback edition.

David once remarked that there was nothing very jolly about the actual writing of a book. It reminded him of that old story of the man banging his head against a brick wall – 'it's so nice when you stop'. What he *did* enjoy was the build-up to the launching of the book. He was meticulous in checking (and often rejecting) dust jacket designs and blurbs. He liked to attend sales conferences where he spent far more time with the 'front line troops', the sales representatives, than the 'generals'. Typical was his first visit to the Putnam office in New York. As he stepped out of the elevator, he was confronted by all the top people lined up to greet him. He asked if he could be excused for a moment – and then found out where the rank and file workers hung out. He spent perhaps a quarter of an hour with them, discovering their names and backgrounds and generally chatting them up with that charming modesty that was partly assumed but largely natural. On all his future visits to the Putnam office during that tour, he would make a point of popping into the workers' quarters to say things like, 'Hello, Sadie, how's your mum's lumbago – better, I hope?'

It paid off in a dramatic way. Just after five o'clock one afternoon when the office was officially closed, there was an urgent phone call from one of the biggest TV chat shows. If a copy of *Moon* could be rushed to the studio right away, David Niven would have the major interview next morning. Every single typist, book-keeper and packer volunteered to take it.

He had a great deal of fun over his choice of titles. Indeed, he and his friend William Buckley used to have a running contest over which of them could come up with the most pointless title that a publisher would accept. But David's titles, however odd, never lacked point. The e.e. cummings poem from which *The Moon's a Balloon* was taken, so movingly read by John Mortimer at the Memorial Service, describes 'all the pretty people' who flock through David's pages. When he and Errol Flynn were making the film of *The Charge of the Light Brigade* at Balaclava, Michael Curtiz, the Hungarian-born director whose command of English was somewhat arbitrary, wanted to show the carnage by a slow tracking shot of riderless horses crossing the screen. 'Bring on the empty horses,' he commanded through his megaphone – and the artist in David stored the phrase away for future use. And finally, an old West Indian nanny who had looked after him and his family on holiday, said as they left, 'Go slowly, come back quickly.' It was to be the title he settled on after various experiments for the last book he was to complete.

He went slowly – and bravely, with that wry self-mocking humour that lasted to the end. His illness affected his vocal chords and it was ironic that the beautiful speaking voice should latterly be so slurred as to be almost indecipherable. Only a few weeks before his death in one of our last telephone conversations, he said, 'Peter Ustinov says I sound like a drunken Russian general – and he ought to know!'

Old men may forget but the books, witty and warm and redolent with the joy of living, will remain.

George Greenfield

London, November 1983

Philip Evans

Editor

On the Road To Scissors Time

I FIRST MET David in February 1973 when I flew to Geneva for lunch. Feeling slightly nervous I took with me some bars of Kendal Mint Cake destined to help 'break the ice'. As if any could need breaking! He was waiting for me on the airport tarmac, accepted my gift as though it were one of the nicest presents which he had ever received, and soon I felt totally soothed by his immense charm. We went to eat at a small restaurant on the northern shore of Lac Leman where over a three-hour meal we discussed the details of a tour which he had agreed to make to coincide with the paperback publication of *The Moon's a Balloon*.

I had been looking forward immensely to our publication of the book ever since joining Coronet Paperbacks as an Editor soon after the rights had been acquired by the then Managing Director, Michael Attenborough. Hardback publishers all the way round the globe had sold copies by the busload and we were terribly grateful to David for making time in his busy schedule to help promote our edition.

In the April he came over for the actual tour: an opening reception at the Savoy in London followed by visits to Manchester, Edinburgh and Birmingham. It must have been an exhausting business paying visits within only four days to centres so far apart but David proved to be an inspiring person with whom to travel and to work. Alongside these receptions, of course, came time which had to be spent giving interviews to local press, radio and television: all arranged by the Publicity Manager, Stella Courtney. Publication of any book in paperback form can often appear to be 'second-best' coming as it does months after the original appearance of the title but throughout David succeeded in making interviews interesting and found new stories to give them a quality of freshness. A true professional throughout.

He would often ring me subsequently whenever he was in London and on several occasions I would write to either Switzerland or France giving him the sales figures: 'We have sold a million and a half in the last three months' and so on. It was in the second week, in February 1975, that Lady Luck intervened, however. During the first days I read and relished a typescript of *Bring On the Empty Horses* which had been sent over by Hamish Hamilton. That was the stroke of Good Fortune. Ill Fortune was close behind, however, because driving home from work one evening (it would have to be February 14th) my car skidded on a wet road and smacked into a lamp-post.

I spent approximately four months in a coma but whenever he was in town David would telephone the hospital to enquire into my condition and after I had woken up used to send me messages of good cheer. In fact he paid a visit to see me when he came over for the hardback publication of *Bring On the Empty Horses*, but ill fortune struck for the second occasion. When he called I was in another part of the hospital doing physiotherapy and was most upset to return to my ward and be told by the Sister that he had been. Eighteen months later, however, when the book appeared in its paperback form, David took time off from doing interviews to pay a visit to my home in Chiswick and his subsequent letters often made remarks of encouragement: 'It was a joy to see you and I would not have missed it for anything'; '*please* keep up with those dull exercises because they seem to have done miracles for you already'; 'poor old chum ... keep going and, as sure as fate, you will be back in the front line again'.

In May 1976 he had written me an uplifting letter which later continued 'Our *Horses* ran beautifully in hardback on both sides of the Atlantic ... it's a better book than *Moon*, I believe, though it was a bastard to do. I think it will have more appeal because *Moon* was only about me and lots of people don't like me! This time the poor sods have more choice ... keep going and get well soon so we can take another of our famous trips with Stella. But this time like General De Gaul (*sic*) I shall require blood banks every 100 yards of the route!'

In the November of 1977, however, I heard from The Connaught informing me about the very serious car accident in which Kristina had been involved and explaining that all David's time was bound up with filming and flying to Switzerland. Later David himself wrote that he had been unable to think of anything else. As soon as she started to become better, however, and his worries considerably lessened, he was able once more to think clearly

David on tour
with his editor,
Philip Evans, and
Stella Courtney.

168

about his writing. In the October of 1978 I received a letter saying he would be back in England before Christmas. 'If you can face it I'd love to come and see you and also pick your brain about my non-book which is still a large piece of paper with 'Chapter 1' written on it. Irwin Shaw told me if I had some good characters and some good locations, the characters would write the story for me. All I can say is that Irwin is a liar! I sit for hours picking my nose and getting nothing down on paper. However I shall continue to pick and hope for the best.'

Those characters and locations eventually came to him and in the October of 1980 David rang and asked me to do a first reading of a novel which he had written and judge whether it was 'publishable' (his word!). A fairly sizeable chunk of what was later to be *Go Slowly, Come Back Quickly* duly arrived which I much enjoyed and about which I wrote five pages of comments. David's response came a month later from a hotel in New York. 'It must have been very difficult seeing only a portion of the horror to make any sense of it!!! Obviously the book needs lots of work ... I'm just getting it all down and looking forward to "scissors time" enormously ... Doubleday are publishing in October so I hope to finish it by end of Feb. Forgive haste ... one foot on a plane, the other on a banana peel.'

In the May of 1982 I sent David a short book which I had written to do with the World Cup (Football not Cricket) for which he was very grateful but his letter of July told me for the first time about his illness. 'Forgive marking-ink pen – I have been struck down by a strange nervous disease which among other things fucks me up (as they say on MAD. AVE.) "gripwise".' Later in the same letter he went on to complain of it being so frustrating 'when some of the machinery begins to wear out! I always thought *that* was reserved for *old* farts but I sense that now young farts of 72 are coming into the firing-line and I *do* so resent it!!!'

He sent me a post-Christmas card in the January of 1983 which said that he was 'struggling with a new novel but it is very tough because the regime I am on gives me so little time to sit down and concentrate. Also I have a sizeable block.' In the last letter which he sent me in June 1983 he said that he was happy to be home, was 'pressing on' and finished by sending his fondest love to us all.

Early in his life David found the key to that magic secret of doing the simple things beautifully and the beautiful things simply. Family, films, friends were his world and for these his generous love seemed to have no limits. Aside from his ever-cheerful and admiring exhortations to me to push on with the punishing therapy were his mad dashes from filming in England to and from Switzerland where his darling daughter Kristina lay horribly injured.

An inimitable raconteur who much enjoyed jokes at his own expense,

A kiss for an autograph – Niv at a signing session for *The Moon's a Balloon* in April 1973.

David's boyish wonder at having written bestsellers was truly captivating. Much of his work was in the film world where hyperbole is often the norm and where calumny and recrimination can sometimes be commonplace, but these emotional niceties were not for him. He looked for the best in people and, searching, found it: he loved life and the little, important things of life so that it returned his love; and he left the world a richer place for his bright presence.

Let his compatriot, Robbie Burns, have the last word with his simple message to John Lapraik:

'The social, honest friendly man whate'er he be,
'Tis he fulfils great Nature's plan and none but he.'

Philip

London, December 1983

Maggie Smith

Rescued on the Nile

I HAD THE pleasure of working with David on three films, *Murder By Death, Death on the Nile* and what proved to be his last picture, *Ménage à Trois* (later retitled *Better Late Than Never*.) He was, as the title of this book says, a Gentleman, and I remember an example of this when we were making *Death on the Nile*.

I was appearing as Rosalind in *As You Like It* in Canada in October 1977. Immediately the curtain fell on the last performance I had to dash by car to Toronto Airport in order to fly all the way to Egypt where filming had already started. I was naturally anxious for a smooth journey and no complications.

The flight was longer and more exhausting than I expected. And when I finally reached Cairo I found that all my luggage was missing! And that night, I was given a hotel room without a lock on the door so *anyone* could walk in or out!

Next day, when I made the final leg of my flight to Luxor where the unit was working, I felt like 'Death on the Nile' itself ...

But then a miracle! At the airport, waiting to meet me was David – cool, smiling and immaculate as always, with a large bunch of flowers in his arms and a bottle of champagne on ice!

It was *so* typical of him! I didn't bother to explain about my missing luggage, I simply burst into tears!

Maggie Smith

Petworth, Sussex
December 1983

Overleaf: With Maggie Smith in *Murder by Death* (1976).

The Films of
David Niven
1932–1982

A Complete Filmography of Fifty Fabulous Years

ALL THE WINNERS (London Film Company, 1932)
Starring: Allan Jeayes, Muriel George, Cyril Chamberlain, and as an uncredited extra, David Niven.
Produced and directed by Bunty Watts.
Screenplay by R. G. White from a story by Nat Gould.
A friend named Priscilla Weigall, daughter of Sir Archie Weigall, who thought David was 'good looking enough to be a movie actor' got him an introduction in 1932 to Bunty Watts, a producer at Sound City Studios in Hertfordshire, which lead to his very first screen appearance as an extra in this thirties melodrama about the horse racing fraternity. Allan Jeayes, a farmer turned actor who had scored something of a hit in the film *The Ghost Train* (1932) and was on his way to becoming a popular British star of the screen, played a man with an eye for winners who attracts the attention of some unscrupulous punters. They try to trap him into helping them in a devious plot to fix a race by threatening his girlfriend. The film was notable for some fine horse racing sequences, and David made his fleeting appearance as one of a crowd of people in a paddock scene. 'Greatly to Priscilla's disappointment,' David wrote later in *The Moon's A Balloon*, 'I was not immediately signed to a million-pound contract and returned to Netheravon (the Army Barracks where he was serving as a professional Army officer) in time for parade on Monday morning.'

Some of Niv's films hit the bullseye – others were less successful . . . but all were entertaining.

CLEOPATRA (Paramount, 1934)
Starring: Claudette Colbert, Henry Wilcoxon, Warren William, Gertrude Michael, C. Aubrey Smith, and David Niven again uncredited as an extra.
Produced and directed by Cecil B. De Mille.
Screenplay by Waldemar Young and Vincent Lawrence.
It was Cecil B. De Mille, one of the great film-makers of Hollywood, who gave the nervous young man from England hoping to find fame and fortune in the film capital, his first bit-part in this sumptuous retelling of the love affair of Mark Antony and the Egyptian Queen. The picture was photographed on an epic scale by De Mille using thousands of extras, among whom was David who had registered himself at the Central Casting Agency as 'Anglo Saxon type, Number 2008'. His part, though, was anything but in this mould as he recalled in *Bring On the Empty Horses*, 'I was one of a thousand "extras" naked except for a loincloth, and as I was being constantly belaboured with special "hurtproof" whips, I gathered that I was a slave and the film was probably *Cleopatra*.' Despite such an inauspicious beginning, David and Cecil B. De Mille were to become friends and work on several later projects together.

LAW OF THE PAMPAS (Paramount, 1935)
Starring: William Boyd, George 'Gabby' Hayes, Russell Hayden, Barbara Britton and David Niven (a Mexican – uncredited).
Produced by Harry Sherman; directed by Aubrey Scotto.
Screenplay by Harrison Jacobs based on the characters created by Clarence E. Mulford.
As a registered 'extra' David secured work on a number of films during the spring and early summer of 1934, the majority of which were Westerns. According to one statement of his the number he appeared in was twenty-seven, and as the work usually involved little more than a day's filming (for which he would receive the princely sum of $2.50) this is not beyond the realms of possibility. Only in this Hopalong Cassidy film, though, has he been positively identified, playing a Mexican cowboy seen riding across the pampas complete with tall hat and flowing poncho. David had himself tried for the part of Hopalong Cassidy which was to halt the decline in the career of William Boyd and turn him into one of the most famous of all the cowboy heroes. The films also marked a turning point in David's career, for in June 1934 he was offered a contract by Sam Goldwyn.

WITHOUT REGRET (Paramount, 1935)
Starring: Elissa Landi, Paul Cavanagh, Frances Drake, Kent Taylor, David Niven.
Produced by B. P. Fineman; directed by Harold Young.

Screenplay by Doris Anderson and Charles Brackett, from the play *Interference* by Roland Pertwee and Harold Dearden.

David's first film in which he received a listing in the credits. He also spoke his first screen line, 'Goodbye, my dear' to Elissa Landi (playing his sister), who is on her way to China where capture by bandits and rescue by an intrepid American airman are only the prelude to some tortuous affairs of the heart.

BARBARY COAST (Goldwyn-UA, 1935)
Starring: Miriam Hopkins, Edward G. Robinson, Joel McCrea, Walter Brennan, Brian Donlevy, David Niven.
Produced by Samuel Goldwyn; directed by Howard Hawks.
Screenplay by Charles MacArthur and Ben Hecht, from the book by Herbert Asbury.

Another one-line appearance for David, as a tough Cockney sailor who declares 'Orl rite – I'll go', but is still pitched out of the window of a brothel in San Francisco. This colourful, star-studded film of a young girl unsuspectingly dragged into vice during the Gold Rush of 1850 and becomes the top call girl of the Barbary Coast was both a critical and financial success.

A FEATHER IN HER HAT (Columbia, 1935)
Starring: Pauline Lord, Basil Rathbone, Louis Hayward, Billie Burke, David Niven.
Produced by Everett Riskin; directed by Alfred Santell.
Screenplay by Lawrence Hazard from the novel by I. A. R. Wylie.

By one of those strange twists of fate, the first film which gave David a chance to play the central figure in a scene cast him as a literary man, a young poet, Leo Cartwright, who is guaranteed to enliven any party. So nervous was he, however, that director Alfred Santell briefed the cast and crew to applaud David at the end of the first take – however bad it was. Mistakenly thinking he had genuinely impressed his fellow workers, David never looked back. The film, though, about a struggling writer who finally creates a hit play, was generally considered too sentimental to succeed.

SPLENDOUR (Goldwyn-UA, 1935)
Starring: Miriam Hopkins, Joel McCrea, Paul Cavanagh, Helen Westley, Billie Burke, David Niven.
Produced by Samuel Goldwyn; directed by Elliot Nugent.
Screenplay by Rachel Crothers.

David's first attempt at the kind of part that became associated with him: the handsome waster prepared to dally with love and not above a little crookedness if the occasion demanded. As the wastrel grandson of a society matron

179

whose family has fallen on hard times and is now trying to restore their fortunes by a profitable marriage, he only succeeds in frustrating the plan.

ROSE MARIE (MGM, 1936)
Starring: Jeanette MacDonald, Nelson Eddy, Reginald Owen, Allan Jones, James Stewart, David Niven.
Produced by Hunt Stromberg; directed by W. S. Van Dyke.
Screenplay by Frances Goodrich, Albert Hackett and Alice Duer Miller from the musical play by Otto A. Harbach and Oscar Hammerstein II.
Although this picture was enormously successful, David as a wealthy playboy whose attentions are rebuffed by the heroine in favour of the handsome Canadian mountie, did little to enhance his film career. He looked ill-at-ease in the part, and was almost totally ignored in the reviews which lauded the two main stars and hailed the arrival of another – the young James Stewart.

PALM SPRINGS (Paramount, 1936)
Starring: Frances Langford, Sir Guy Standing, Ernest Cossart, Spring Byington, David Niven.
Produced by Walter Wanger; directed by Aubrey Scotto.
Screenplay by Joseph Fields based on the novel, *Lady Smith* by Myles Connolly.
David followed *Rose Marie* with another musical, playing a weak-willed millionaire under the thumb of a formidable aunt who is nearly inveigled into marriage by a bright young thing set on saving her impoverished father from his creditors. Again, the picture did little to help David's career, although it did reunite him with the director from his Western 'extra' days.

DODSWORTH (Goldwyn-UA, 1936)
Starring: Walter Huston, Ruth Chatterton, Paul Lukas, Mary Astor, David Niven.
Produced by Samuel Goldwyn; directed by William Wyler.
Screenplay by Sidney Howard based on the novel by Sinclair Lewis.
David played a smooth and calculating young Englishman who turns the head of a motor tycoon's wife while on an Atlantic crossing, in this superb adaptation of Sinclair Lewis's famous novel about infidelity and passion. The picture won an Academy Award, high praise for Walter Huston, and gave David the chance of working with one of Hollywood's great directors, William Wyler. He was, though, cruelly treated by the *Detroit Free Press* film critic who wrote, 'In this picture we were privileged to see the great Samuel Goldwyn's latest discovery – all we can say about this actor (?) is that he is tall, dark and not the slightest bit handsome.' David had this review

framed and hung it on the wall of his lavatory!

THANK YOU, JEEVES (20th Century-Fox, 1936)
Starring: Arthur Treacher, Virginia Fields, David Niven, Lester Matthews.
Produced by Sol M. Wurtzel; directed by Arthur Greville.
Screenplay by Joseph Hoffman and Stephen Gross based on the novel by
P. G. Wodehouse.
The first picture in which David was one of the stars – perfectly cast as
Wodehouse's charming but ineffective Bertie Wooster, opposite Arthur
Teacher's immaculate Jeeves. Wooster becomes unwittingly involved with a
beautiful but mysterious young woman being pursued by gunmen and it
takes all Jeeves's ingenuity to extract his master and the young woman from
a dangerous although occasionally hilarious situation. The critics, almost to
a man, agreed that Niven was everyone's idea of Bertie Wooster.

David Niven, the archetypal Englishman, playing one in his first starring role as Bertie Wooster in *Thank You, Jeeves* with Virginia Fields as the sleeping heroine and Arthur Teacher, the redoubtable Jeeves.

THE CHARGE OF THE LIGHT BRIGADE (Warner Bros, 1936)
Starring: Errol Flynn, Olivia de Havilland, Patric Knowles, Nigel Bruce, David Niven, Spring Byington, E. E. Clive.
Produced by Hal B. Wallis; directed by Michael Curtiz.
Screenplay by Michael Jacoby and Rowland Leigh based on the poem by Alfred Tennyson.
The first of David's blood and thunder epics with his friend and (for a time) house-mate, Errol Flynn, in a highly sensationalised version of the immortal charge on the north-west frontier of India. Enormous publicity accompanied the making of the picture – including charges of cruelty to horses which resulted in Warner Bros being fined – and it proved a great box office success. Though never in the forefront of the action, David was praised for his playing of the dashing Captain Randall.

BELOVED ENEMY (Goldwyn-UA, 1936)
Starring: Merle Oberon, Brian Aherne, Karen Morley, Jerome Cowan, David Niven.
Produced by George Haight; directed by H. C. Potter.
Screenplay by John Balderston, Rose Franken and William Brown Meloney from an original story by John Balderston.
Against the grim background of the Irish troubles of 1921, David plays the secretary of Lord Athleigh, a top British civil servant sent to Dublin with his daughter to try and reach a peace settlement. The girl falls in love with one of the Irish insurgent leaders and nearly jeopardises the proposed peace plan until duty overcomes love. Although the story somewhat distorted history, the acting of all the leading characters – David among them – was complimented on both sides of the Atlantic.

WE HAVE OUR MOMENTS (Universal, 1937)
Starring: Sally Eilers, James Dunn, Mischa Auer, Thurston Hall, David Niven.
Produced by Edmund Grainger; directed by Alfred L. Werker.
Screenplay by Bruce Manning and Charles Grayson from an original story by Charles F. Belden and Frederick Stephani.
Once again David was cast as a debonair crook who with his three partners pretend to be a group of society folk while busy robbing their unsuspecting victims. On the verge of being discovered, the quartet plant their loot on an innocent schoolteacher who finds herself branded as being one of their gang, before the love of a detective hot on the trail finally puts matters to rights. Though entertaining, the picture was hardly a success.

THE PRISONER OF ZENDA (Selznick-UA, 1937)

Starring: Ronald Colman, Madeleine Carroll, Douglas Fairbanks Jnr, Mary Astor, C. Aubrey Smith, Raymond Massey, David Niven.

Produced by David O. Selznick; directed by John Cromwell and W. S. Van Dyke.

Screenplay by John Balderston, Donald Ogden Stewart and Wells Root, from the novel by Anthony Hope.

The famous Anthony Hope story of a plot to prevent King Rudolph of Ruritania from being crowned and thereby forfeiting his throne, mixed with the love of the princess for the man who impersonated her betrothed, was perhaps more effectively served by this version than any of the others. Ronald Colman was strikingly effective in the dual role of king and impersonator, while Douglas Fairbanks Jnr, Aubrey Smith and David Niven were all hailed for their strong supporting roles. *The Prisoner of Zenda* is one of the few of David's early films that remains truly effective to this day.

Working with two of the doyens of Hollywood, C. Aubrey Smith and Ronald Colman, in *The Prisoner of Zenda.*

DINNER AT THE RITZ (New World-20th Century-Fox, 1937)
Starring: Annabella, David Niven, Paul Lukas, Romney Brent, Francis L. Sullivan.
Produced by Robert T. Kane; directed by Harold Schuster.
Screenplay by Roland Pertwee and Romney Brent.
This picture brought David home to Britain for the first time to star opposite 20th Century-Fox's new discovery from France, Annabella. He played a debonair investigator who helps his beautiful co-star in tracking down the man who has murdered her wealthy banker father. The film was shot at Denham Studios and offered some glamorous settings – as well as giving David his most challenging role to date.

BLUEBEARD'S EIGHTH WIFE (Paramount, 1938)
Starring: Claudette Colbert, Gary Cooper, Edward Everett Horton, David Niven.
Produced and directed by Ernst Lubitsch.
Screenplay by Charles Brackett and Billy Wilder based on a play by Alfred Savoir.
Cast as a suave Frenchman, Albert de Regnier, David made an ideal foil for Gary Cooper as Michael Brandon, an American multi-millionaire as successful in business as he is unsuccessful with women. With seven failed marriages behind him, he begins the pursuit of an eighth, only to be seemingly rejected in favour of the David Niven character. But the wiles of women are many and varied, and this time it is 'Bluebeard's' turn to come to heel.

FOUR MEN AND A PRAYER (20th Century-Fox, 1938)
Starring: Loretta Young, Richard Greene, George Sanders, David Niven, C. Aubrey Smith, John Carradine, William Henry, Alan Hale.
Produced by Kenneth MacGowan; directed by John Ford.
Screenplay by Richard Sherman, Sonya Levien and Walter Ferris based on the novel by David Garth.
This was a more dramatic role for David after a string of lightweight parts, and also gave him the valuable experience of being directed by John Ford. He was one of the four brothers seeking to restore the reputation of their murdered soldier father who has been accused of causing the death of some of his troops. In the pursuit of an international munitions ring which was at the back of the murder, the four young men – David in particular – were offered fine opportunities to demonstrate their talents and each showed why a long and fruitful career lay ahead of him.

THREE BLIND MICE (20th Century-Fox, 1938)
Starring: Loretta Young, Joel McCrea, David Niven, Stuart Erwin, Marjorie Weaver.
Produced by Raymond Griffiths; directed by William A. Seiter.
Screenplay by Brown Holmes and Lynn Starling from a play by Stephen Powys.
Three poor country girls who inherit a small fortune decide to use it as the bait to net themselves wealthy husbands – and one of those who falls for the ploy is David Niven. However, his wealthy playboy image is only a front, and the sister who has fallen for him is torn between the lure of money and true love. Inevitably, love triumphs. This was David's second appearance with Loretta Young who had been instrumental in getting him into the film business.

DAWN PATROL (Warner Bros, 1938)
Starring: Errol Flynn, David Niven, Basil Rathbone, Donald Crisp, Melville Cooper.
Produced by Hal B. Wallis; directed by Edmund Golding.
Screenplay by Seton I. Miller and Dan Totheroh, based on an original story, *Flight Commander* by John Mark Saunders and Howard Hawks.
David was joined again by his friend Errol Flynn and the accomplished Basil Rathbone in this First World War air drama, skilfully directed by Edmund Golding. As two young pilots trying to outdo each other through feats of drinking on the ground and reckless bravery in the air, Niven and Flynn were ideally paired and though their heroics pay the inevitable price – only Niven survives to shoulder the responsibility of carrying on the war – the pace and style of the film delighted audiences. Film critics, too, were unanimous in their praise, and in several instances David actually stole the best notices from his close friend.

WUTHERING HEIGHTS (Goldwyn-UA, 1939)
Starring: Merle Oberon, Laurence Olivier, David Niven, Flora Robson, Donald Crisp, Hugh Williams, Leo G. Carroll.
Produced by Samuel Goldwyn, directed by William Wyler.
Screenplay by Ben Hecht and Charles MacArthur from the novel by Emily Brontë.
Although some of Hollywood's finest talents were brought to bear on this production, David was initially totally opposed to playing the part of Edgar Linton which he considered 'unactable'. Certainly bringing this classic novel to the screen presented enormous problems, but once David had conquered his initial reluctance he brought a depth of characterisation and emotion to his part which proved to anyone who might have nursed doubts that he was

an actor of wide ranging skills. David forged what proved a lifelong friendship with his fellow Englishman, Laurence Olivier, during the making of this picture.

BACHELOR MOTHER (RKO Radio, 1939)

Starring: Ginger Rogers, David Niven, Charles Coburn, Frank Albertson, E. E. Clive.
Produced by B. G. De Sylva; directed by Garson Kanin.
Screenplay by Norman Krasna from an original story by Felix Jackson.
A young shopgirl mistakenly believed to be the mother of an orphaned baby becomes emotionally involved with the son of a department store tycoon. Despite the endless complications presented by the baby – not the least of them that the man is the father of the girl's surprise package – their love blossoms in a story both warm and witty. Ginger Rogers played the girl with considerable panache, and such was David's mastery of the tycoon's son, that the London *Observer* newspaper wrote enthusiastically, 'As for Mr Niven, he is growing, film by film, into one of the best romantic comedians in the cinema.' *Bachelor Mother* also proved enormously popular with audiences in Britain where it lightened the gloom of the early days of September 1939 just before the outbreak of World War II.

THE REAL GLORY (Goldwyn-UA, 1939)

Starring: Gary Cooper, Andrea Leeds, David Niven, Reginald Owen, Broderick Crawford, Kay Johnson.
Produced by Samuel Goldwyn; directed by Henry Hathaway.
Screenplay by Jo Swerling and Robert R. Presnell from the novel by Charles L. Clifford.
A dramatic and colourful story of some beleaguered American troops in the Philippines holding out against savage local tribesmen. Gary Cooper is at the heart of the action as a doctor, and David as Lt McCool has to rebuff a fanatical attack on the fort where the Americans are trapped, and in the bloody and heroic stand gives his life to save the others.

ETERNALLY YOURS (Wagner-UA, 1939)

Starring: Loretta Young, David Niven, Hugh Herbert, Billie Burke, C. Aubrey Smith, Broderick Crawford, Zasu Pitts.
Produced by Walter Wanger; directed by Tay Garnett.
Screenplay by Gene Towne, Graham Baker and John Meeham.
Partnered once again by Loretta Young, David plays a stage magician, The Great Arturo, whose love of the bright lights conflicts with his wife's plans of a quiet life in a little house in the country. Parting company when David goes off on a world tour, he returns sadder and wiser and performs one last daring

—and almost fatal—stunt, before settling happily for the domesticity he originally rejected.

RAFFLES (Goldwun-UA, 1939)

Starring: David Niven, Olivia de Havilland, Dame May Whitty, Douglas Walton, E. E. Clive.

Produced by Samuel Goldwyn; directed by Sam Wood and William Wyler. Screenplay by John Van Druten and Sydney Howard, based on the book, *The Amateur Cracksman* by E. W. Hornung.

The role of the gentleman burglar who plays cricket by day and robs the homes of the wealthy by night was tailor-made for David Niven, and he, for his part, was keen to play it. With a Scotland Yard detective hot on his trail, Raffles is nearly unmasked in this story when he falls in love with the sister of his friend, Bunny, and risks a daring robbery to save his financially embarrassed pal. Niven's portrayal of Raffles remains to this day the best remembered of several versions of the story.

Another rare still of Niv and his friend Errol Flynn in *Dawn Patrol,* somewhat bemused by the German Von Meuller (Carl Esmond).

THE FIRST OF THE FEW (British Aviation Pictures, 1942)
Starring: Leslie Howard, David Niven, Rosamund John, Roland Culver, Anne Firth.
Produced and directed by Leslie Howard.
Screenplay by Anatole de Grunwald and Miles Malleson from an original story by Henry C. James and Kay Strueby.
This was David's first film in two years, having returned home to Britain in 1939 on the outbreak of World War II to enlist. It told the story of the development of the Spitfire plane which was to play such a crucial role in the war and of its designer's (Leslie Howard's) struggle with officialdom to get its revolutionary capabilities accepted, along with the bravery of the test pilot (Niven) who nursed it through its first hair-raising trials. David was given special leave to make this basically patriotic picture, and was acclaimed by *The Scotsman*'s film critic who said, 'Niven's performance as the test pilot is one of the best he has done.'

THE WAY AHEAD (Two Cities, 1944)
Starring: David Niven, Raymond Huntley, William Hartnell, Stanley Holloway, John Laurie, Peter Ustinov, Tessie O'Shea.
Produced by John Sutro and Norman Walker; directed by Carol Reed.
Screenplay by Eric Ambler and Peter Ustinov from a story by Eric Ambler. For the second of his wartime films, David, who was now a Lieutenant-Colonel in the Army, turned to a military subject and the training of a bunch of raw recruits into a fighting force of soldiers. David could draw on his own experience in playing Lt Jim Perry and supported by some of Britain's best character actors, the result was a film both instructive in Army methods and entertaining in its vivid account of men at war. As the basic idea for the film had been his own, David turned in a heartfelt and authentic performance, aided by the skilful direction of Carol Reed.

A MATTER OF LIFE AND DEATH (J. Arthur Rank, 1945)
Starring: David Niven, Roger Livesey, Raymond Massey, Kim Hunter, Marius Goring, Richard Attenborough.
Produced, directed and written by Michael Powell and Emeric Pressburger. An experimental and controversial film, it was nevertheless chosen as the first Royal Command Film Performance after the war and attracted reviews which raged against its apparent anti-British sentiments on one hand to claims that it was 'clearly one of the three or four best films of the year' on the other. David played a crashing bomber pilot who, because of a mix-up in Heaven, survives the accident, only to be accosted in hospital by an emissary of the spirit world who insists he joins them. Able to get his case settled by arbitration, and by now deeply in love with a girl, he makes such a strong

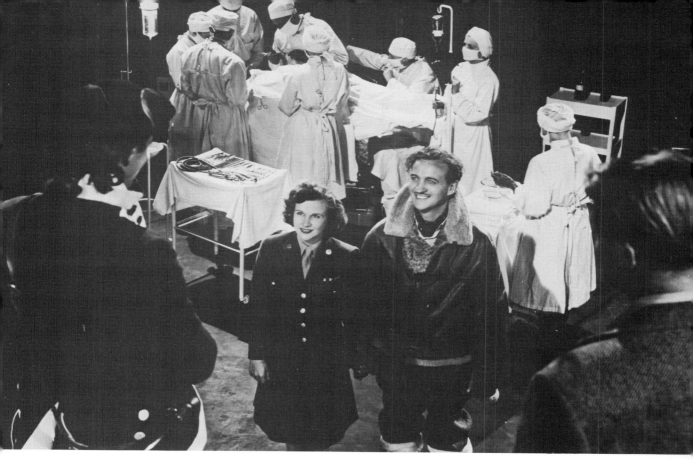

case that he is allowed an extension of life by the emissary and all ends happily.

Niv's first post-war film, *A Matter of Life and Death,* which was also the first Royal Command Performance picture. His co-star was Kim Hunter.

THE PERFECT MARRIAGE (Paramount, 1946)
Starring: Loretta Young, David Niven, Nona Griffith, Eddie Albert, Virginia Field, Charles Ruggles, Zasu Pitts.
Produced by Hal Wallis; directed by Lewis Allen.
Screenplay by Leonard Spigelgass based on a play by Samson Raphaelson.
David's return to Hollywood also reunited him with Loretta Young in a film which was, frankly, awful. The pair played a couple going through a mid-marriage crisis who seem stubbornly set on divorce until friends prove to them that their love runs deeper than a temporary upset and they are happily thrown back into one another's arms. The best that reviewers could find to say about David's performance was that it was 'sheepish'!

MAGNIFICENT DOLL (Universal Pictures, 1946)
Starring: Ginger Rogers, David Niven, Burgess Meredith, Horace McNally, Frances Williams.
Produced by Jack H. Skirball and Bruce Manning; directed by Frank Borzage.

Screenplay by Irving Stone.

Cast as the American traitor, Aaron Burr, opposite his friend Ginger Roger's Dolly Madison, David considered this story 'gibberish' and must surely have wondered if his return to Hollywood had been worthwhile after two such bad films. He played the suave but rotten Burr who schemes to set himself up as Emperor of the Americans, and is only saved from a lynch-mob and allowed to flee the country because of a passionate defence by the woman (Ginger Rogers) who once loved him.

THE OTHER LOVE (Enterprise Productions-UA, 1947)

Starring: Barbara Stanwyck, David Niven, Richard Conte, Gilbert Roland, Joan Lorring.

Produced by David Lewis; directed by André de Toth.

Screenplay by Ladislas Fodor and Harry Brown from the story *Beyond* by Erich Maria Remarque.

Another lack-lustre film with David playing a doctor in a Swiss sanatorium who nurses a brilliant concert pianist (Barbara Stanwyck) back to health and falls in love with her, only to see her rush into another man's arms when she thinks he is responsible for the death of one of his patients. Happily, though, the couple are reunited, but their joy is short-lived for the pianist dies one evening while the doctor quietly tries to play one of her favourite piano pieces.

THE BISHOP'S WIFE (Goldwyn-RKO, 1947)

Starring: Cary Grant, Loretta Young, David Niven, Monty Woolley, Gladys Cooper, Elsa Lanchester.

Produced by Samuel Goldwyn; directed by Henry Koster.

Screenplay by Robert E. Sherwood and Leonard Bercovici from the novel by Robert Nathan.

A picture beset with problems from start to finish. David went about his work with a heavy heart having just lost his first wife in a tragic accident, and his load was not lightened when Samuel Goldwyn sacked the original director, pulled down the sets, and had the script rewritten after two weeks' shooting had been completed. David played a bishop more concerned with plans for a new cathedral than the welfare of his parishioners and, more particularly, his own family. Seeking guidance from above, he is sent an angel in the debonair shape of Cary Grant who captivates the bishop's wife (Loretta Young), but does not transgress the bounds of decency before leaving the household all happily content once more. Despite another outcry from reviewers, *The Bishop's Wife* was selected as the second Royal Command Film and proved a great box office success.

Niv, curiously cast as a man of the cloth in *The Bishop's Wife.*

190

BONNIE PRINCE CHARLIE (London Films, 1948)
Starring: David Niven, Margaret Leighton, Judy Campbell, Jack Hawkins, Finlay Currie, John Laurie.
Produced by Edward Black; directed by Anthony Kimmins.
Screenplay by Clemence Dane.
This film has been described as one of the most disastrous British films ever made. Taking over a year to complete, it went hugely over budget, was listlessly acted to put it mildly, and was in turn unmercifully savaged by the critics. David had made it clear from the start that he did not want to make the film, and indeed in his blond wig and chocolate box costumes he looks ill at ease from start to finish. Even with his Scottish associations, David could do nothing to save the story of Bonnie Prince Charlie's unsuccessful rise against the English, and must have cringed with shame when he read reviews like that of the *Sunday Graphic* which wrote that 'David Niven looked as much at home among the Highlanders as a goldfish in a haggis'.

ENCHANTMENT (Goldwyn-UA, 1948)
Starring: David Niven, Teresa Wright, Evelyn Keyes, Farley Granger, Leo G. Carroll.
Produced by Samuel Goldwyn; directed by Irving Reis.
Screenplay by John Patrick from the novel, *Take Three Tenses* by Rumer Godden.
Some skilful use of make-up allowed David to play an ageing general reminiscing on his past in this story set in World War II where a family gathering releases some old skeletons from the past. Playing the old soldier as a young man, David was once again able to demonstrate his skill at tackling the cool, handsome character and did much to restore his reputation after the débâcle of *Bonnie Prince Charlie*.

A KISS IN THE DARK (Warner Bros, 1949)
Starring: David Niven, Jane Wyman, Victor Moore, Broderick Crawford, Wayne Morris.
Produced by Jack L. Warner; directed by Delmer Davies.
Screenplay by Harry Kurnitz from a story by Everett and Devery Freeman.
Yet another unhappy experience for David playing a concert pianist who is dominated by an unscrupulous agent and brought to the verge of ruin until saved for a simpler though less financially-rewarding life by the love of a pretty but unsuccessful model (Jane Wyman). The *News of the World* just shook its head and asked, 'What on earth are they doing with that fellow's career?'

THE ELUSIVE PIMPERNEL (London Films, 1949)
Starring; David Niven, Margaret Leighton, Cyril Cusack, Jack Hawkins,
Arlette Marchal.
Produced, directed and written by Michael Powell and Emeric Pressburger,
based on the novel, *The Scarlet Pimpernel* by Baroness Orczy.
The famous story of the nobleman who disguises himself to snatch victims
from the guillotine during the terrors of the French Revolution was a
tremendous box office success although David was never completely happy
with his portrayal of the remarkable Sir Percy Blakeney. He was, though,
well supported by Margaret Leighton playing his wife, and Cyril Cusack as
the sinister Chauvelin relentlessly pursuing the elusive Pimpernel.

This was one of
many surprising
moments from
*The Elusive
Pimpernel.*

A KISS FOR CORLISS (Strand Production-UA, 1949)
Starring: Shirley Temple, David Niven, Tom Tully, Virginia Welles, Darryl Hickman.
Produced by Colin Miller; directed by Richard Wallace.
Screenplay by Howard Dimsdale based on a story by F. Hugh Herbert.
Cast opposite the former child star, Shirley Temple, now twenty-one years old and a mother but still playing teenage parts, the picture was to prove a disaster for David. It was also the last film he made under contract to Samuel Goldwyn. The tritest possible story had David as a womaniser who is unwittingly used by a canny lawyer to deflect his pretty daughter (Shirley Temple) from what he considers an unsuitable romance. David looked as unhappy in his part as did Miss Temple as a bobbysoxer, and the *Sunday Chronicle* bemoaned his fate: 'Poor David Niven! Only a really great star could save a picture in which he scarcely appears at all!'

THE TOAST OF NEW ORLEANS (MGM, 1950)
Starring: Kathryn Grayson, Mario Lanza, David Niven, J. Carrol Naish, Rita Moreno.
Produced by Joe Pasternack; directed by Norman Taurog.
Screenplay by Sy Gomberg and George Wells.
In a picture that was unashamedly set up to promote the new singing star, Mario Lanza, David was cast as Jacques Riboudeaux, an opera company impressario, who is prepared to sacrifice his star (Kathryn Grayson), whom he loves in a desultory sort of fashion, to the charms of Lanza in order to capture his undoubted raw talent for his company. It was David's first film as a freelance actor.

HAPPY GO LOVELY (Associated British-RKO, 1950)
Starring: David Niven, Vera-Ellen, Cesar Romero, Bobby Howes, Diane Hart, Gordon Jackson.
Produced by Marcel Helman; directed by Bruce Humberstone.
Screenplay by Val Guest based on a story by F. Damman and Dr H. Rosenfield.
David achieved excellent press notices in his third musical in which he played B. G. Bruno, a millionaire Scottish greeting card king who is inveigled into putting his money into a musical show about to be launched in Edinburgh. Vera-Ellen, as the apple of his eye and the reason for staking his hard-earned cash, unwittingly thinks him a fraud, and is on the verge of ruining both David and the show before the glory of love opens her eyes to the real situation.

SOLDIERS THREE (MGM, 1951)
Starring: Stewart Granger, Walter Pidgeon, David Niven, Robert Newton, Cyril Cusack, Greta Gynt, Dan O'Herlihy.
Produced by Pandro S. Berman; directed by Tay Garnett.
Screenplay by Marguerite Roberts, Tom Reed and Malcolm Stuart Boylan based on the book by Rudyard Kipling.
A stylish and colourful Indian adventure loosely based on Rudyard Kipling's famous story, it found David cast as Captain Pindenny assigned with the difficult task of controlling or at least keeping apart three wild soldiers in his infantry brigade who are much given to fighting and drinking. This, and coping with rebellious local tribesmen, lead to some hilarious incidents culminating in acts of bravery which delighted audiences and critics alike.

APPOINTMENT WITH VENUS (British Film Makers, 1951)
Starring: David Niven, Glynis Johns, Barry Jones, Kenneth Moore, Noel Purcell.
Produced by Betty E. Box; directed by Ralph Thomas.
Screenplay by Nicholas Phipps from the book by Gerrard Tickell.
Filmed on the lovely Channel Island of Sark, the film related the daring wartime plan of snatching a pedigree cow called Venus from underneath the noses of the occupying German troops. In charge of the raiding party is David as Major Valentine Morland, again drawing on his real-life experience, to give this officer a believable air and the right amount of charm to enlist the aid of the islanders to remove their prize beast and win the heart of a pretty local ATS girl (Glynis Johns).

THE LADY SAYS NO! (Ross-Stillman-UA, 1951)
Starring: Joan Caulfield, David Niven, James Robertson Justice, Lenore Lonergan.
Produced by Frank Ross and John Stillman Jnr; directed by Frank Ross.
Screenplay by Robert Russell.
Another undistinguished film in which David plays a photographer who sets out to take some portraits of an authoress of a bestselling book preaching to women about the wiles of men. It takes repeated attempts to get pictures of the beautiful but truculent lady (Joan Caulfield), but David's ultimate reward is her love and the downfall of her philosophy.

THE MOON IS BLUE (Holmby-UA, 1953)
Starring: William Holden, David Niven, Maggie McNamara, Tom Tully, Dawn Adams.
Produced by Otto Preminger and F. Hugh Herbert; directed by Otto Preminger.

Screenplay by F. Hugh Herbert from his play *Camera*.

After virtually two years of inactivity following his break with Samuel Goldwyn, this film reinvigorated David's career. It was the first film made by Otto Preminger as an independent producer, and immediately outraged certain authorities in America by the use of such words as 'mistress', 'seduce' and 'virgin' – with the result that it had to be released without a Seal of Decency. In England, it was some years before it could be shown. Nevertheless the scandal guaranteed success at the box office, and David's excellent reviews were topped-off when he was awarded a Golden Globe for the best comedy performance of the year as a suave charmer who almost outsmarts William Holden for the hand of the demure young TV actress played by Maggie McNamara. The picture also heralded the first signs of a crumbling in the famous Hollywood Production Code and marked a major step forward in what could be seen and heard on the screen.

THE LOVE LOTTERY (Ealing Studios, 1953)
Starring: David Niven, Peggy Cummins, Anne Vernon, Herbert Lom, Gordon Jackson, Felix Aylmer.
Produced by Monja Danischewsky; directed by Charles Crichton.
Screenplay by Harry Kurnitz from a story by Charles Neilson Gattey and Zelma Bromley-Moore.
A lighthearted comedy in which David played Rex Allerton, a dashing Hollywood film star anxious about his fame who agrees to take part in a 'Love Lottery' in which the first prize will be a week spent with him. Endeavouring to fix the result so that the girl he loves wins ahead of all his worldwide fans who also enter, nearly ends in disaster until his real personality as a rather weak individual makes him desirable only to . . . the girl he loves. The *Daily Mail* declared enthusiastically, 'David Niven has his best part for a long time and rises splendidly to the occasion.'

HAPPY EVER AFTER (Associated British, 1954)
Starring: David Niven, Yvonne de Carlo, Barry Fitzgerald, George Cole, A. E. Matthews.
Produced and directed by Mario Zampi.
Screenplay by Jack Davies, Michael Pertwee and L. A. G. Strong.
David played an out-and-out bounder, Jasper O'Leary, who inherits an Irish estate and then proceeds to milk it and the local population for all they are worth. These normally docile souls decide the only solution to their problem is to do away with Jasper, and they are on the verge of succeeding after several farcical attempts, when a new will comes to light which states that Jasper can be removed quite simply if he proves unpopular.

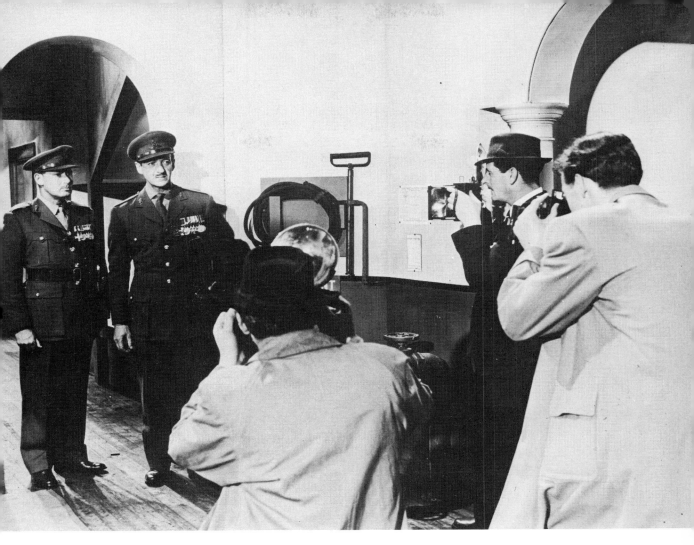

CARRINGTON, VC (Romulus Films, 1954)
Starring: David Niven, Margaret Leighton, Noelle Middleton, Laurence
Naismith, Clive Morton, Raymond Francis.
Produced by Teddy Baird; directed by Anthony Asquith.
Screenplay by John Hunter from the play by Dorothy and Campbell Christie.
A strikingly successful film for David in which he played Major Carrington,
VC, an Army man of impeccable record who is forced to 'borrow' money to
pay off a debt and at the same time compromises a young WRAC officer –
resulting in his court martial. He is found guilty and is ordered to be
dismissed from the service: until a last-minute confession by a telephonist
who listened in to one of his telephone calls and can substantiate his claim to
be not guilty. In America the film ran into trouble because of the relationship
of the major with the young girl, but the critics loved the film, the *Spectator*
in particular enthusing that Niven 'gives one of the best performances of his
career'.

Back into Army
uniform for
his splendid
performance in
Carrington VC
with co-star
Raymond Francis.

THE KING'S THIEF (MGM, 1955)
Starring: Ann Blyth, Edmund Purdom, David Niven, George Sanders, Roger Moore, John Dehner.
Produced by Edwin H. Knopf; directed by Robert Z. Leonard.
Screenplay by Christopher Knopf from a story by Robert Hardy Andrews.
Yet another costume drama which did little for David's career, casting him as the villainous Duke of Brampton who uses his position of trust with Charles II to root out alleged traitors, enriching himself with their confiscated wealth and lands. When he runs up against a gentleman highwayman (Edmund Purdom) and his lady (Ann Blyth), the black-hearted villain gets his richly deserved comeuppance. The film, though, was given an emphatic thumbs down by critics and audiences alike.

THE BIRDS AND THE BEES (Gomalco-Paramount, 1956)
Starring: George Gobel, Mitzi Gaynor, David Niven, Reginald Gardiner, Harry Bellaver.
Produced by Paul Jones; directed by Norman Taurog.
Screenplay by Sidney Sheldon from the story *The Lady Eve* by Preston Sturges.
Cast as an unscrupulous cardsharper called Colonel Harris, David did much to carry this film which was actually set up to introduce an enormously successful television personality, George Gobel, to cinema audiences. He was crafty and dashing as he endeavoured to part the foolish Gobel from his money, and then movingly believable when his daughter (Mitzi Gaynor) falls for the poor sap she was also helping to lure into the trap.

AROUND THE WORLD IN EIGHTY DAYS (Michael Todd-UA, 1956)
Starring: David Niven, Cantinflas, Robert Newton, Shirley MacLaine, Charles Boyer, Ronald Colman, Noel Coward, Marlene Dietrich, John Mills, Frank Sinatra.
Produced by Michael Todd; directed by Michael Anderson.
Screenplay by James Poe, John Farrow, S. J. Perelman from the novel by Jules Verne.
The role of world-traveller Phileas Fogg was one that David told producer Mike Todd he would play 'for nothing' – and was almost made to do so! The picture was a lavish, hugely expensive spectacular chock full of stars, yet none outshone David who gave what remains one of the most memorable of all his screen performances. His dash from the Reform Club in London around the world, replete with excitement and adventure, thrilled audiences and critics, and earned the film an Oscar as Best Picture. 'David Niven,' the *Financial Times* chorused with the rest of the press, 'is superb.'

A blonde Niv!
Looking
understandably
less than
enthusiastic about
his forthcoming
role in *The Birds
and the Bees.*

THE SILKEN AFFAIR (Dragon Films, 1956)
Starring; David Niven, Genevieve Page, Ronald Squire, Wilfred Hyde-White, Richard Wattis.
Produced by Douglas Fairbanks and Fred Feldkamp; directed by Roy Kellino.
Screenplay by Robert Lewis Taylor from a story by John McCarten.
A chance meeting with a dazzling French beauty (Genevieve Page), turns a brilliant but boring accountant (David Niven) into something of a rascal when he begins to fiddle the books of some of his clients, turning one failing company into a success, and bringing another to the verge of ruin. Discovered at last, he escapes a jail sentence, but returns to his wife and his former life, a chastened but wiser man. Surrounded by some strong British character actors, David gave a brilliantly comic performance, and was described by *Time and Tide* as 'just about the best living exponent of English farce'.

OH, MEN! OH, WOMEN! (20th Century-Fox, 1957)
Starring: Dan Dailey, Ginger Rogers, David Niven, Barbara Rush, Tony Randall.
Produced, directed and written by Nunnally Johnson.
David plays a psychiatrist to the wealthy of Manhattan in this film in which his life is turned upside down when one of his female clients confesses that her husband has a fixation for the doctor's fiancée. When a second client also reveals the same problem, poor Dr Alan Coles loses his cool – and because of it his fiancée. Happily, though, a reconciliation is worked out by one of those twists of fate which are the inevitable outcome of films like this. It marks no kind of landmark in David's career.

THE LITTLE HUT (MGM, 1957)
Starring: Ava Gardner, Stewart Granger, David Niven, Walter Chiari, Finlay Currie.
Produced by F. Hugh Herbert and Mark Robson; directed by Mark Robson.
Screenplay by F. Hugh Herbert from the play by Andre Roussin adapted by Nancy Mitford.
A love triangle on a desert island where David as Henry Brittingham-Brett has been shipwrecked with Sir Philip Ashlow and his wife Susan (Stewart Granger and Ava Gardner) and then finds himself the object of the lady's affections. But Susan's intentions are mostly to rekindle her husband's long dormant interest in her, and she goes to the extent of a mock divorce ceremony to inflame his jealousy. The arrival of a handsome ship's chef into the party further complicates the issue, but finally drives the estranged couple back into each other's arms. The picture was generally panned by the critics, several of them finding David's performance 'the one saving grace'.

MY MAN GODFREY (Universal Pictures, 1957)
Starring: June Allyson, David Niven, Jessie Royce Landis, Robert Keith, Eva Gabor.
Produced by Ross Hunter; directed by Henry Koster.
Screenplay by Everett Freeman, Peter Berneis and William Bowers based on a novel by Eric Hatch.
David played to perfection the part of an apparent tramp picked up by a New York society girl and turned into a butler, only to have to confess later when confronted by someone from his past that he is actually an impoverished Austrian count. June Allyson, as the girl, falls in love with him and then frustrates the intentions of certain other members of her family who would have him fired. In the end he earns the everlasting gratitude of the father of the family by saving him from bankruptcy and thereby gets the hand of his society girl.

BONJOUR TRISTESSE (Columbia Pictures, 1957)
Starring: Deborah Kerr, David Niven, Jean Seberg, Mylene Demongeot, Juliette Greco, Walter Chiari, Martita Hunt.
Produced and directed by Otto Preminger.
Screenplay by Arthur Laurents from the novel by Françoise Sagan.
Cast as the middle-aged playboy father Raymond, opposite Jean Seberg as his approving daughter, Cecile, David brought a special panache to his part in this screen version of the notorious French bestselling novel. Deborah Kerr, a long-time friend, was Anne, the older, more mature woman who tries to rescue him from the endless round of shallow relationships with pretty, empty-headed girls only to be driven to distraction and a sad death which leaves its mark on both Raymond and Cecile, making them only too painfully aware that it was their selfishness that caused the tragedy. Although not without its moments of conflict, the relationship between David and Otto Preminger did much to give the film its undoubted style.

SEPARATE TABLES (Clifton-UA, 1958)
Starring: Deborah Kerr, Rita Hayworth, David Niven, Wendy Hiller, Burt Lancaster, Gladys Cooper, Felix Aylmer.
Produced by Harold Hecht; directed by Delbert Mann.
Screenplay by Terence Rattigan and John Gay from the play by Terence Rattigan.
Arguably David's finest screen performance – certainly the one which earned him his only Oscar as Best Actor playing the deceptively charming Major Pollack, a guest in a genteel private hotel who regales everyone with tales of his war exploits and forms a relationship with the timid Sibil Railton-Bell (Deborah Kerr). When scandal intrudes on her life, and the major is also

exposed as a liar who never rose higher than a lieutenant and is also accused of molesting women, the two are drawn together in mutual shame and weakness. David's performance was hailed as a masterpiece, and there was credit, too, for the deeply realised character played by Deborah Kerr.

ASK ANY GIRL (MGM, 1959)
Starring: David Niven, Shirley MacLaine, Gig Young, Rod Taylor, Jim Backus, Claire Kelly.
Produced by Joe Pasternak; directed by Charles Walters.

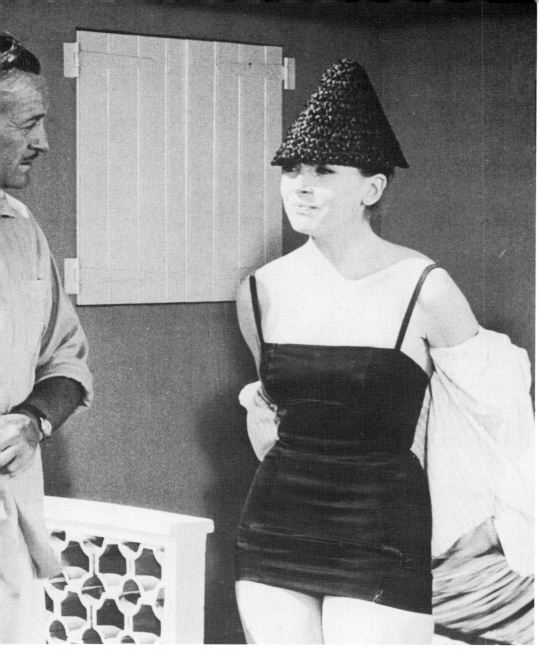

Another moment of humour with Deborah Kerr and Jean Seberg while making *Bonjour Tristesse.*

Screenplay by George Wells based on a novel by Winifred Wolfe.

David enjoyed working again with Shirley MacLaine who played an innocent girl from the country who falls foul of the pitfalls of big city life – not to mention the lecherous attentions of several men. That is until David as a somewhat straightlaced (for a change) research company boss takes her under his wing and despite himself, falls in love with her. The picture was funny, often hilarious, and the newspapers were full of praise for David, including the *Sunday Times* who said, 'David Niven, all polish and impeccable timing, makes every gesture tell.'

HAPPY ANNIVERSARY (Fields Productions Inc-UA, 1959)
Starring: David Niven, Mitzi Gaynor, Carl Reiner, Loring Smith, Monique Van Vooren.
Produced by Ralph Fields; directed by David Miller.
Screenplay by Joseph Fields and Jerome Chodorov based on their own play.
While they are celebrating their thirteenth wedding anniversary, Chris and Alice Walters (David and Mitzi Gaynor) confess under the influence of champagne to her shocked parents that they were going to bed together before they were married. This conversation is also overheard by the couple's children who promptly proceed to make capital out of the fact and nearly drive the couple apart. Only the news that Alice is pregnant again saves the foundering marriage from final collapse. Sadly, the picture was not as good as the original witty and gently shocking play which had scored such a success by knocking some of America's most cherished institutions.

PLEASE DON'T EAT THE DAISIES (MGM, 1960)
Starring: Doris Day, David Niven, Janis Paige, Spring Byington, Richard Haydn.
Produced by Joe Pasternak; directed by Charles Walters.
Screenplay by Isobel Lennart from the book by Jean Kerr.
A former university professor, Lawrence Mackay (David Niven), leaves his teaching post to become a New York theatre critic and immediately becomes embroiled in a crisis of conscience when forced to review an awful play by an old friend. The subsequent review makes them enemies, but establishes his reputation – which goes to his head. When his wife (Doris Day) moves the family from New York and takes part in an amateur dramatic presentation of a play he wrote years before, he comes to appreciate the other side of the coin and the balance of his life, as well as domestic harmony, is speedily restored.

THE GUNS OF NAVARONE (Open Road Films-Columbia, 1961)
Starring: Gregory Peck, David Niven, Anthony Quinn, Stanley Baker, Anthony Quayle, Richard Harris, Bryan Forbes.
Produced by Carl Foreman and Cecil Ford; directed by J. Lee Thompson.
Screenplay by Carl Foreman from the novel by Alistair MacLean.
A spectacular action film which took two years to make and was if anything even more costly and more widely publicised than David's earlier epic, *Around the World in Eighty Days*. He played Corporal Miller, one of a group of Allied saboteurs dispatched to blow up some highly fortified German guns on the Greek island of Navarone which threaten all military operations in the area. The all-star cast of extremely professional actors brought real tension and excitement to the picture which culminated in one

A fine portrait from one of Niv's favourite films, *The Guns of Navarone.*

204

of the noisiest and most spectacular explosions ever seen on the screen. And David, along with Gregory Peck and Anthony Quinn, was singled out for his 'brilliant performance'.

THE BEST OF ENEMIES (De Laurentis-Columbia, 1961)
Starring: David Niven, Alberto Sordi, Michael Wilding, Harry Andrews, Noel Harrison, Bernard Cribbens.
Produced by Dino De Laurentis; directed by Guy Hamilton.
Screenplay by Jack Pulman from a story by Luciano Vincenzoni.
An interesting role for David in this multi-national picture in which he was called upon to satirise just the kind of British Army officer he had played in so many of his previous films – and he did it with polish and skill. He plays Major Richardson who by force of circumstances is thrown into an alliance with some Italian soldiers in Ethiopia in 1941. With the fortunes of each group fluctuating as the war around them takes one turn then another, they come to form a grudging respect for each other which even the final imprisonment of the Italians does not diminish. *Time* magazine heralded the general approval, 'Sandhurst-trained David Niven never lets down the light comedy side of officership.'

THE CAPTIVE CITY (Maxima Films, 1962)
Starring: David Niven, Ben Gazarra, Michael Craig, Martin Balsam, Lea Massari, Daniela Rocca.
Produced and directed by Joseph Anthony.
Screenplay by Guy Elmes, Marc Brandel and Eric Bercovici from the novel, *The Captive City* by John Appleby.
In another multi-national production, David played Peter Whitefield, called upon to lead a group of civilians trapped in a hotel in Athens in World War II and under fire from Greek army and partisan groups. Trying to stave off the attack until British troops arrive, the group is also threatened by a traitor in their midst, but Niven – ever the stalwart – manages to save them all and even organise an escape to safety.

THE ROAD TO HONG KONG (Melnor-UA, 1962)
Starring: Bing Crosby, Bob Hope, Joan Collins, Dorothy Lamour, Robert Morley, Jerry Colonna, David Niven, Frank Sinatra, Dean Martin, Peter Sellers.
Produced and directed by Norman Panama.
Screenplay by Norman Panama and Melvin Frank.
Another of the seemingly endless 'Road' films starring Bing Crosby and Bob Hope, with David appearing in this one as a guest star making a fleeting appearance playing a Tibetan monk!

GUNS OF DARKNESS (Cavalcade-Warners, 1962)
Starring: Leslie Caron, David Niven, James Robertson Justice, Richard Pearson, Eleanor Summerfield.
Produced by Ben Kadish and Thomas Clyde; directed by Anthony Asquith.
Screenplay by John Mortimer from the novel, *Act of Mercy* by Francis Clifford.
Caught in the turbulence of a revolutionary coup in a South American republic, Tom Jordan (David Niven), a man bored with his life and at odds with his wife (Leslie Caron), finds himself suddenly at the centre of another drama when he comes across the badly wounded president of the country who has just been deposed. Determined to help him escape from certain death, Jordan risks his own life in a mad dash to the border and only manages to succeed in his mission by overcoming his natural reluctance to kill. Once again David took the accolades, the *Financial Times* declaring that he 'seems continually to improve as an actor'.

55 DAYS IN PEKING (Bronston-Allied Artists, 1963)
Starring: Charlton Heston, David Niven, Ava Gardner, Robert Helpmann, Flora Robson, Harry Andrews, Elizabeth Sellars.
Produced by Samuel Bronston; directed by Nicholas Ray.
Screenplay by Philip Yordan and Bernard Gordon.
This was the film David called 'an open-air Western in Chinese', and he played the redoubtable Sir Arthur Robertson who has to rally the besieged foreigners caught in Peking during the bloody Boxer Rebellion in 1900. The spectacular movie which cost over four million pounds to make, caught the high drama of the trapped garrison and their brave efforts to resist the marauding yellow hordes – including a brilliant underground assault on the Chinese arsenal. The picture proved widely popular and David was commended for his performance, which *The Times* said, he played 'with his habitual authority'.

THE PINK PANTHER (Mirisch-UA, 1964)
Starring: David Niven, Peter Sellers, Robert Wagner, Capucine, Claudia Cardinale, Brenda de Banzie, John Le Mesurier, Michael Trubshawe.
Produced by Martin Jurow; directed by Blake Edwards.
Screenplay by Maurice Richlin and Blake Edwards.
This picture provided David with his one and only appearance with his long-time Army friend turned actor, Michael Trubshawe. It also united him with another friend, Peter Sellers, Niven playing the aristocratic sportsman, Sir Charles Lytton, to Sellers' accident prone, bumbling detective inspector Jacques Clouseau. Sir Charles is, in fact, also a daring jewel thief known as 'The Phantom' and he has set his sights on a valuable and dazzling jewel

Just a few of the
star-studded cast
from *55 Days in
Peking* — Niv with
Elizabeth Sellars,
Robert Helpmann,
Charlton Heston
and Ava Gardner.

known as the Pink Panther. After a series of hilarious adventures, Sir Charles is actually unmasked by the detective, but at his trial manages to switch the blame from himself to Inspector Clouseau. The unhappy policeman is left sitting in jail while Sir Charles makes good his escape: but, as the world now knows, the exploits of Sellers' madcap detective had only just begun . . .

BEDTIME STORY (Lankershim-Pennebaker-Universal, 1964)
Starring: Marlon Brando, David Niven, Shirley Jones, Dody Goodman, Aram Stephen.
Produced by Stanley Shapiro; directed by Ralph Levy.
Screenplay by Stanley Shapiro and Paul Henning.
Despite the actor's reputation for being difficult, David found working with Marlon Brando a delight, and in later years he often spoke kindly of the usually moody method actor being a skilful comedian. David played a playboy to Brando's Army corporal in a comedy about their activities as very different but equally successful con-men praying on beautiful women. The pair in fact join forces to try and fleece an American heiress (Shirley Jones), but love takes over and while Brando steals away with the girl, David just as happily goes off to plan his next exploit.

WHERE THE SPIES ARE (MGM, 1965)
Starring: David Niven, Françoise Dorleac, Cyril Cusack, John Le Mesurier, Nigel Davenport, Eric Pohlman, Noel Harrison.
Produced by Val Guest and Steven Pallos; directed by Val Guest.
Screenplay by Val Guest, Wolf Mankowitz and James Leasor from the novel, *Passport to Oblivion* by James Leasor.
This was intended to be the first of a series of spy thrillers featuring David as James Leasor's character, Dr Jason Love, a country doctor who served in intelligence work during World War II, and is occasionally brought out on new assignments. Sadly, though the film was popular at the box office and David was totally convincing as a secret agent far removed from James Bond, there were no sequels. In this film, Dr Love is called upon to foil an assassination plot against a pro-British Arab prince, and does so after some hair-raising brushes with Russian agents and a romantic entanglement with the lovely Françoise Dorleac.

LADY L (Concordia-MGM, 1965)
Starring: Sophia Loren, Paul Newman, David Niven, Claud Dauphin, Phillipe Noiret, Cecil Parker, Peter Ustinov.
Produced by Carlo Ponti; directed by Peter Ustinov.
Screenplay by Peter Ustinov from the novel by Romain Gary.

Peter Ustinov made a delightful and at times highly satirical film from Romain Gary's story about the life of the famous Lady Lendale of the title (Sophia Loren) who rose from being the laundress in a brothel to become the wife of an eccentric English aristocrat (David Niven). The story is told in the form of flashbacks from Lady L's eightieth birthday party, and although the critics were far from happy at seeing an aged Sophia Loren or Paul Newman as a French anarchist, they to a man considered David's performance as the sad and often cynical lord 'a piece of vintage Niven'.

EYE OF THE DEVIL (Filmways-MGM, 1966)
Starring: Deborah Kerr, David Niven, Donald Pleasence, Edward Mulhare, Flora Robson, Emlyn Williams, Sharon Tate, David Hemmings.
Produced by Martin Ransohoff and John Calley; directed by J. Lee Thompson.
Screenplay by Robin Estridge and Dennis Murphy from the novel, *Day of the Arrow* by Philip Loraine.
This picture brought David and his friend Deborah Kerr back together again in a story far removed from the genteel decay of *Separate Tables* – plunging them into a world of horror and secret sacrificial rituals. Strange forces also seemed to have been at work right from the start of the filming, because the original leading lady, Kim Novak, was injured after eight weeks' work, and had to be replaced by Deborah Kerr at the cost of all the completed footage. The couple are drawn into the web of a group of satanists poisoning a country estate with their evil practices, and only escape at the cost of their son. The picture itself always appeared somehow doomed, and the unfortunate Sharon Tate as a maid with sinister magical powers was herself soon to meet a terrible death at the hands of Charles Manson and his weird blood cult.

CASINO ROYALE (Famous Artists-Columbia, 1967)
Starring: Peter Sellers, Ursula Andress, David Niven, Orson Welles, Joanne Pettet, Woody Allen, Deborah Kerr, William Holden, John Huston, George Raft.
Produced by Charles K. Feldman and Jerry Bresler; directed by John Huston, Ken Hughes, Val Guest, Robert Parrish, Joe McGrath, Richard Talmadge and Anthony Squire.
Screenplay by Wolf Mankowitz, John Law and Michael Sayers from the novel by Ian Fleming.
This was an unashamed, not to say spectacular, send-up of the James Bond movies with David playing an ageing Bond in retirement who is called up for one last assignment against the evil agents of SMERSH who are wreaking havoc in the highlands of Scotland. Bond's son and daughter come to the aid

of David's splendid Sir James, and the pyrotechnics of his performance are only matched by the tremendous special effects. The other star names race in and out of the story almost too fast to be spotted: a fact which can probably be blamed as much on the profusion of directors as the complexity of the plot!

THE EXTRAORDINARY SEAMAN (MGM, 1968)
Starring: David Niven, Faye Dunaway, Alan Alda, Mickey Rooney, Jack Carter, Barry Kelly.
Produced by Edward Lewis; directed by John Frankenheimer.
Screenplay by Phillip Rock and Hal Dresner from a novel by Phillip Rock. Another satire on World War II with David playing Lt Commander Finchhaven, RN, in which he gathers a motley crew of four American seamen and a girl (Faye Dunaway) to help him refloat an abandoned Royal Navy ship in the Philippines on the promise that he will transport them to Australia. Once at sea, Finchhaven reveals that he is actually a ghost sent back to earth to redeem his unhappy naval career and that he plans to do so by sinking a Japanese cruiser. Reluctantly the crew decide to help him – only to learn after successfully completing the mission that the war is already over and poor Finchhaven has still to redeem himself.

PRUDENCE AND THE PILL (20th Century-Fox, 1968)
Starring: Deborah Kerr, David Niven, Robert Coote, Irina Demick, Joyce Redman, Judy Geeson, Keith Michell.
Produced by Kenneth Harper and Ronald Kahn; directed by Fielder Cook and Ronald Neame.
Screenplay by Hugh Mills from his novel, *Camera*.
Another partnering of David and Deborah Kerr, this time in a comedy on the touchy subject of contraception and the varied effects on a couple and their relations by the discovery that the womenfolk are all on the pill – hence extra-marital activities are suspected. These reach a climax in a series of divorces, some hasty remarriages, and pregnancies all round: a direct result of some vindictive swapping of pills with aspirins. The film was neither a success with the paying public nor the critics.

THE IMPOSSIBLE YEARS (Marten-MGM, 1968)
Starring: David Niven, Lola Albright, Chad Everett, Ozzie Nelson, Christina Ferrare, Jeff Cooper.
Produced by Lawrence Weingarten; directed by Michael Gordon.
Screenplay by George Wells from a play by Bob Fisher.
A film about the Generation Gap, with David as Dr Jonathan Kingsley, a psychiatrist specialising in teenagers, who predictably cannot control or

influence his seventeen-year-old daughter. Trying to encourage a new relationship with her, he only succeeds in filling his life with hippies and artists and reaching the edge of despair. When all seems lost, the girl reforms herself in her own way, and the relieved Dr Kingsley has to face the fact that there is much the old can learn from the young. There can be no denying that this was an awful picture, and *The People* unceremoniously declared it was, 'David Niven in his worst ever film'.

BEFORE WINTER COMES (Windward-Columbia, 1969)
Starring: David Niven, Topol, Anna Karina, John Hurt, Anthony Qualye, Ori Levy.
Produced by Robert Emmett Ginna; directed by J. Lee Thompson.
Screenplay by Andrew Sinclair from the novel, *The Interpreter* by Frederick L. Keefe.
A return to uniform for David in a much more demanding role as Major Giles Burnside, an officer in Austria at the end of World War II faced with the difficult task of placing displaced persons in refugee camps or returning them to an uncertain fate in the East. At the heart of the story is Janovic (Topol) who acts as interpreter between the major and his interviewees, and then becomes his rival for the affections of a local girl (Anna Karina). When Burnside learns that Janovic is actually a Russian deserter, he overrules his conscience and instead of sending him to the West returns him to certain execution in Russia. The critics were pleased to be able to say something complimentary about David again, the *Daily Mail* praising him for 'wavering subtly between impersonal military authority and personal weakness'.

THE BRAIN (Gaumont International-Paramount, 1969)
Starring: David Niven, Jean-Paul Belmondo, Bourvil, Eli Wallach, Silvia Monti.
Produced by Alain Poire; directed by Gerard Oury.
Screenplay by Gerard Oury, Marcel Jullian and Daniel Thompson.
David remained in uniform – though deceptively so – for this international co-production playing a colonel in the British Army who also happens to be 'The Brain', the mastermind of the British Great Train Robbery. He is now planning to snatch the entire military funds of NATO, and although he is partly frustrated by some other villains with the same idea in mind, does get his hands on the money and is just about to smuggle it out of Europe to America in a huge replica of the Statue of Liberty when disaster brings all his plans to nought. Without David and his mastery of comedy and irony, this picture would certainly have been another disaster: and so all the critics thought.

THE STATUE (Shaftel, 1970)
Starring: David Niven, Virna Lisi, Robert Vaughn, Ann Bell, John Cleese, Tim Brooke-Taylor, Hugh Burden.
Produced by Anis Nohra; directed by Rod Amateau.
Screenplay by Alec Coppel and Denis Norden from the play, *Chip, Chip, Chip* by Alec Coppel.
David was back in his best gentleman's outfit as Professor Alex Bolt, the inventor of a new universal language which wins him a Nobel Prize. It also earns his sculptress wife Rhoda (Virna Lisi) a commission to immortalise him in a huge statue to be placed in Grosvenor Square. But what she produces is a giant replica *in the nude* with physical endowments the poor professor knows are certainly not his! So whose are they? The search for the unexpected answer brings in politicians and secret service men and leads David a merry dance before his peace of mind – and his marriage – are finally saved.

KING, QUEEN, KNAVE (Wolper Pictures, 1972)
Starring: Gina Lollobrigida, David Niven, John Moulder Brown, Mario Adorf.
Produced by David L. Wolper; directed by Jerzy Skolimowski.
Screenplay by David Seltzer and David Shaw from the novel by Vladimir Nabokov.
This typically complex Nabokov story cast David as a formerly dashing World War II captain who remained in Munich after the war, married a beautiful refugee (Gina Lollobrigida) and built himself a successful business. When a young nephew from England who has just lost his parents is thrust into their world, a mixture of sexual undertones between the boy and the wife and the man's half-formed thoughts of making him his heir, lead to an explosive finale in which the destinies of the king, queen and knave are settled. Despite the style and grace of the film, it failed to match the expectation of the pairing of Niven and Lollobrigida and the much-vaunted directing skills of Jerzy Skolimowski.

VAMPIRA (World Film Services, 1973)
Starring: David Niven, Teresa Graves, Peter Bayliss, Jennie Linden, Nicky Henson, Bernard Bresslaw, Freddie Jones, Frank Thornton.
Produced by Jack H. Weiner; directed by Clive Donner.
Screenplay by Jeremy Lloyd.
The screen had never had a Count Dracula quite like David Niven in this spoof horror movie with the blood-drinking vampire turned into a witty and debonair English nobleman. His mission is to revive his beloved countess (Teresa Graves) who lies undead back in Transylvania and to this end he sets about collecting blood from the beautiful girls of London – with some

unexpected results when he inadvertently gives his wife a sample taken from a gorgeous black girl. The count gets the right corpuscles in the end, but the comedy gets blacker and blacker as things go on (if you'll excuse the pun). The critics thought it a 'glorious idea' to have David play Dracula, and perhaps only because the film appeared amidst a host of other horror films of varying degrees of quality and nastiness, did it fail to make the impact it deserved.

THE CANTERVILLE GHOST (HTV, 1974)
Starring: David Niven, James Whitmore, Lynne Frederick, Flora Robson, Audra Lindley, Maurice Evans.
Produced by Timothy Burrill; directed by Walter Miller.
Screenplay by Robin Miller based on the story by Oscar Wilde.
From a vampire, David next found himself playing a ghost in a version of Oscar Wilde's famous story of an American family who take over an English stately home which has a spectre-in-residence. But the visitors are far from frightened of David's rather benevolent old ghost and indeed he has a hard time haunting at all, so plagued is he by the family's two sons. Help in the form of the beautiful daughter finally puts all to rights in the spirit world. David's enjoyment while making this comic story is evident in every scene.

PAPER TIGER (Lloyd-MacLean Films, 1974)
Starring: David Niven, Toshiro Mifune, Hardy Kruger, Ronald Fraser, Jeff Corey, Patricia Donahue, Kurt Christian.
Produced by Euan Lloyd; directed by Ken Annakin.
Screenplay by Jack Davies.
A marvellous performance by David as an English teacher named Walter Bradbury who is coaching a Japanese ambassador's son on a Pacific island when he suddenly finds himself caught up in an assassination attempt which puts to the test stories he has told of great wartime bravery. When he and the boy are captured by guerillas, Bradbury collapses and reveals the true nature of his so-called heroism: he is a coward at heart. Yet even in the most timid of men there lurks unexpected strength when a real crisis presents itself, and he and the boy manage to escape — only to be relentlessly pursued and avoid re-capture at the very last moment. It was a moving performance by David, built on a lifetime of playing characters with hidden secrets, and was warmly applauded by the critics, including Dilys Powell who wrote, 'David Niven plays with his unfailing elegance and that touch of pathos which is his especial gift.' Her only regret, she said, was that 'I wish only that someone could find the perfect role for Mr Niven.'

NO DEPOSIT, NO RETURN (Walt Disney, 1975)

Starring: David Niven, Barbara Feldon, Kim Richard, Brad Savage, Don Knotts, Darren McGavin, Vic Tayback.

Produced by Ron Miller and Joseph McEveety; directed by Norman Tokar. Screenplay by Arthur Alsberg and Don Nelson from a story by Joseph McEveety.

The first of two thriller comedies David made for Disney, playing a rich and at times absent-minded grandfather who has two young and rather wilful children (Kim Richard and Brad Savage) dumped on him for their holidays, and then lead him a merry dance by pretending to be kidnapped by two bungling safe-breakers in order to extract a ransom from him. David, aware of what is really going on, refuses to pay a cent for the little monsters and uses the 'kidnap' as a means of giving them a little taste of their own medicine. Although generally disliked by the critics, Margaret Hinxman of the *Daily Mail* wrote, 'Any film starring David Niven can't be bad, although I suspect his performance owes more to his own impeccable sense of comedy timing than Norman Tokar's rather laboured direction.'

MURDER BY DEATH (Columbia, 1976)

Starring: Eileen Brennan, Truman Capote, James Coco, Peter Falk, Alec Guinness, Elsa Lanchester, David Niven, Peter Sellers, Maggie Smith.

Produced by Ray Stark; directed by Robert Moore.
Screenplay by Neil Simon.

A superlative performance by David in a splendid comedy film written by Neil Simon and much enjoyed by critics and cinemagoers alike. Truman Capote was cast as Lionel Twain, an eccentric millionaire who invites five famous detective friends to his home – each a parody of a well-known fictional detective – with the promise of a tax-free fortune to whichever one solves a murder he says is to be committed on the stroke of midnight. David played Dick Charleston, 'The Thin Man', with Maggie Smith as his wife; Elsa Lanchester was Miss Marbles; Peter Sellers appeared as Sidney Wang; Peter Falk as Sam Diamond; James Coco as Milo Perrier; and Alec Guinness as a blind butler trying to maintain some sort of order amidst a profusion of disappearing bodies, sinister eyes peering through walls, collapsing ceilings, deadly insects and endless, echoing screams. Penelope Gilliatt led the cheers for the film in the *New Yorker*, 'Never before have been collected in one film such confident wild syntax,' she said, while Arthur Thirkell of the *Daily Mirror* said it was a picture of 'diabolical inventiveness and hilarious mickey-taking'. And with a nice gesture to the past, Margaret Hinxman added, 'Who but David Niven and Maggie Smith could have impersonated Dick and Dora so elegantly – except, of course, William Powell and Myrna Loy?'

CANDLESHOE (Walt Disney, 1977)
Starring: Leo McKern, Jodie Foster, David Niven, Helen Hayes, Vivian Pickles, Vernon Quilligan.
Produced by Ron Miller; directed by Norman Tokar.
Screenplay by David Swift and Rosemary Anne Sisson based on the novel, *Christmas at Candleshoe* by Michael Innes.

David's second film in just over a year for Walt Disney in which he played three roles in one: as a chauffeur, friend and gardener to Lady St Edmund of Candleshoe, one of England's stately homes. Leo McKern was cast as his co-star, a Cockney con-man who takes a New York tomboy (Jodie Foster) from her slum home to England where he passes her off as the missing Fourth Marchioness of Candleshoe in order that she might find the clues to a vast fortune hidden somewhere in the house by a forebear. It was a change for David not to be cast as the con-man and he made the most of his three roles, in particular that of the bewhiskered chauffeur.

DEATH ON THE NILE (EMI, 1978)
Starring: Peter Ustinov, Jane Birkin, Lois Chile, Bette Davis, Mia Farrow, David Niven, Maggie Smith, I. S. Johar, George Kennedy.
Produced by John Brabourne and Richard Goodwin; directed by John Guillermin.

Screenplay by Anthony Shaffer based on the novel by Agatha Christie.
David enjoyed co-starring with his old friend Peter Ustinov in EMI's ten-million-dollar version of Agatha Christie's famous murder mystery. Playing an English lawyer, Colonel Race, he was on hand to watch developments and lend a hand when Hercule Poirot (Ustinov) set out to discover who had killed the haughty American heiress Linette (Lois Chiles) while honeymooning on a Nile steamer. As with any Christie story, virtually everyone on the ship had a good reason for wanting the lady dead, and there are the inevitable twists and turns – not to mention numerous red herrings – before Poirot reveals all. The critics, to a man, praised David for his role as a 'debonair foil for Ustinov', *The Spectator* adding that he was 'his usual immaculate self'.

ESCAPE TO ATHENA (ITC Entertainment, 1979)
Starring: Roger Moore, Telly Savalas, David Niven, Stefanie Powers, Claudia Cardinale, Richard Roundtree, Sonny Bono, Elliott Gould.
Produced by David Niven Jnr and Jack Weiner; directed by George Pan Cosmatos.
Screenplay by Richard S. Lochte II and Edward Anhalt based on a story by Richard S. Lochte and George Pan Cosmatos.
A unique experience for David – working in a film produced by his son, who had followed in his footsteps, though behind the cameras rather than in front of them. The picture was another wartime exploit set in a prisoner of war camp in Greece in 1944. The commandant of the camp (Roger Moore) is actually more interested in excavating works of art on the island than furthering the war and consequently recruits the help of a group of prisoners, led by David as an erudite professor. They naturally have their own ideas about what is to become of any loot, but complications in the form of intervention by Greek resistance fighters and the chance discovery of a secret Nazi missile hideout on the island leads to a literally explosive finale. The *Western Mail* reported that despite it being a generally disappointing film, 'Niven makes his usual suave contribution.'

A NIGHTINGALE SANG IN BERKELEY SQUARE
(S. B. Fisz Productions, 1979)
Starring: Richard Jordan, David Niven, Oliver Tobias, Gloria Grahame, George Baker, Joss Ackland, Elke Sommer, Anthony Heaton, Davy Kaye.
Produced by S. Benjamin Fisz; directed by Ralph Thomas.
Screenplay by Guy Elmes.
Another complete change of pace for David playing the cunning and brilliant mastermind of a gang of twenty-five men who break into an American bank in Berkeley Square in London and steal over thirty million dollars from safety deposit boxes. The story was based on actual events which happened

in 1975 and although all the men were subsequently caught, convicted and given heavy jail sentences (with the exception of the ringleader who escaped from the Old Bailey) it was felt best to disguise them under new names. David had the identity of 'Ivan the Terrible' – 'a kind of London Godfather' he described the part – and particularly enjoyed the filming because he could walk from the Connaught Hotel where he stayed to the main location in Berkeley Square.

A MAN CALLED INTREPID (Lorimer Productions Ltd, 1979)
Starring: Michael York, Barbara Hershey, David Niven, Peter Gilmore, Flora Robson, Gayle Hunnicutt.
Produced by Intrepid Productions; directed by Peter Carter.
Screenplay by David Ambrose based on the book by William Stevenson.
A six-hour television special (for which there were plans at one time to shorten to a one-hour fifty-minute cinema release) about the activities of Sir William Stephenson, a Canadian multi-millionaire with a special knowledge of espionage who was asked by Winston Churchill in 1938 to set up a spy ring with the code name Intrepid. There were memories of his own wartime experiences for David playing Sir William, and he lent style and authority to the role controlling his little group of spies in the maelstrom which was Europe during the Nazi occupation. Their desperate search for clues to the German plan to develop an atomic bomb made for exciting viewing, although certain military figures who had been associated with the actual exploits of Intrepid were less than happy at what they saw as the romanticising and sensationalising of certain elements of the story.

ROUGH CUT (Paramount, 1980)
Starring: Burt Reynolds, Lesley-Anne Down, David Niven, Timothy West, Patrick Magee, Joss Ackland, Isobel Dean, Andrew Ray.
Produced by David Merrick; directed by Don Siegel.
Screenplay by Francis Burns based on the novel, *Touch The Lion's Paw* by Derek Lambert.
David might almost have felt that his career had come full circle in this picture when he was cast as Chief Inspector Willis of Scotland Yard whose burning ambition before he retires is to catch a debonair, elusive jewel thief described as 'an American Raffles in London'. This time it was Burt Reynolds who played the dashing cracksman always keeping just one step ahead of the law, even when he falls under the spell of a high society kleptomaniac (Lesley-Anne Down) who is actually the bait in a trap the chief inspector has set. Although the film had more than its fair share of trouble while being made, and caused David to take his one and only piece of legal action against the makers over his billing, it did earn him excellent reviews,

including one from *Now* magazine which declared, 'David Niven at his most splendidly world-weary, is right out of Burke (Peerage, not Hare).'

THE SEA WOLVES (Uniprom International, 1980)
Starring: Gregory Peck, Roger Moore, David Niven, Trevor Howard, Barbara Kellerman, Patrick Macnee.
Produced by Euan Lloyd; directed by Andrew V. McLagen.
Screenplay by Reginald Rose based on the book, *Boarding Party* by James Leasor.
Another spirited war romp for David cast with two of his closest friends, Gregory Peck and Roger Moore, as members of The Calcutta Light Horse, a bunch of irregular but real-life soldiers who in 1942 took part in one of the most outlandish operations of World War II. Although long past combat age, these veterans commandeered an old ship to knock out a German vessel based in neutral Goa harbour which had been transmitting information about Allied shipping to a German U-Boat waiting out at sea ready to pounce. These remarkable old stagers, with David as a most redoubtable leader, put paid to the raider despite all the odds. In making the picture, Euan Lloyd managed to find a few of the veterans still alive, and Lt Col. Lewis Pugh (played by Gregory Peck in the film) said after the preview, 'It is exciting and entertaining and full of commanding performances' – a view also shared by the majority of critics and cinema audiences.

BETTER LATE THAN NEVER (a.k.a. *Ménage à Trois*)
(Golden Harvest, 1981)
Starring: David Niven, Maggie Smith, Art Carney, Kimberley Partridge, Catherine Hicks.
Produced by David Niven Jnr and Jack Haley Jnr; directed by Bryan Forbes.
Screenplay by Bryan Forbes from an idea by Gwen Davis.
A sadly poignant title for what proved David's last starring role playing a broken-down English musical entertainer opposite Art Carney as a failed photographer. The two men are brought together in France where one or other of them is likely to be the grandfather of a precocious nine-year-old girl who has just been orphaned and left a fortune. Both old-timers had a wartime affair with the little child's grandmother: and one left her pregnant with the girl's mother. Maggie Smith was cast as Anderson, the girl's cynical and amusing nanny, with Catherine Hicks as a delightful beauty named Sable who flirts with David on a beach. Although he was already in the grip of the disease which was to take his life, David threw himself into the role with his usual high spirits and, ironically, considering the problems he was increasingly suffering with his speech, actually *sang* on screen for the first time in his career – a Noël Coward tune, 'I Went To A Marvellous Party'.

David's last screen appearance in *Rough Cut.*

The words were somehow significant of his attitude towards life. He was, as ever, ready to help and encourage his young co-star Kimberley Partridge, and delivered one of his most poignant screen lines at the end of the picture when he told her, 'Don't grow up too quickly.'

THE TRAIL OF THE PINK PANTHER (MGM-United Artists, 1982)
Starring: Peter Sellers, Robert Wagner, Capucine, Joanna Lumley, David Niven, Richard Mulligan, Herbert Lom, Harvey Korman, Graham Stark, Burt Kwouk.
Produced and directed by Blake Edwards.
Screenplay by Maurice Richlin and Blake Edwards.
David's final screen moments were a group of scenes for the latest of Blake Edwards' Pink Panther films. It was a return to the part of Sir Charles Lytton, known as 'The Phantom', a role he had first created in the original Pink Panther movie made in 1964. The basis of the picture was unused footage from earlier Panther films starring Peter Sellers which Blake Edwards linked with new material. Because of David's illness, the film crew came to the South of France to make his scenes which were actually shot 'back-to-back' near the Niven villa at Cap Ferrat in May 1982. However, even though David could act his part, he found increasing difficulty in articulating his lines and most of his dialogue had to be re-recorded by the impressionist, Rich Little. 'He didn't want the world to know he was really ill,' Little said afterwards. 'He just wanted to go on working as always. He was incredibly brave and full of good humour despite the pain.' It was a typical act of the man, and showed for one last time why he will be remembered as one of this century's best loved performers – among both actors and audiences alike.

Acknowledgements

I should like to express my sincere thanks to the following for their help in the writing of this book: John Mortimer, Tommy Phipps, Douglas Fairbanks Jnr, Lauren Bacall, Greg Bautzer, Dame Flora Robson, Lord Olivier, Rt Hon. Lord Hailsham, Phil Gersh, Sir John Mills, Deborah Kerr, Lana Turner, Jerome Chodorov, Brian Doyle, Maggie Smith, Bette Davis, Gregory Peck, Gene Kelly, Bryan Forbes, George Greenfield, Philip Evans, Anthony Quayle, John Doubleday, Charles Foster, S. St John Hartness, Roderick Mann, Bill Lofts, *Express Newspapers* for permission to reprint David Niven's article, 'Dear Trubshawe', *The Times* for the letters to that newspaper in July 1973, the staff of the British Film Institute, The British Museum Newspaper Library and The London Library; and Paramount Pictures, MGM, Columbia, 20th Century-Fox, Warner Bros, Universal Pictures, United Artists, Walt Disney, EMI and Golden Harvest. Colour section – pages 1 and 3: Kobal Collection; page 2: Rex Features; page 4: London Features International. And, particularly, Ralph Fields and David Niven Jnr, for encouragement; and Vivienne Petch who so industriously and enthusiastically helped in gathering the tributes which form the core of this book.

PETER HAINING